Scottish Independence

Weighing Up the Economics

Gavin McCrone

BIRLINN

This edition first published in 2014 by
Birlinn Limited
West Newington House
10 Newington Road
Edinburgh
EH9 1QS

www.birlinn.co.uk

ISBN: 978 1 78027 234 4

British Library Cataloguing-in-Publication Data
A catalogue record for this book is available from the British Library

Typeset by Iolaire Typesetting, Newtonmore
Printed and bound by Grafica Veneta
www.graficaveneta.com

To my family, for whom Scotland's future is important

Contents

Foreword

As the date for a referendum on Scottish independence grows closer, arguments for and against what would amount to the greatest constitutional change in Britain for more than 300 years have grown intense. A sense of something approaching national anxiety can be discerned as Scots of every persuasion seek answers to the fundamental questions that will govern the outcome before they go to the polls in September 2014. Would an independent Scotland be worse or better off? More pertinently, perhaps, would it have the capacity to flourish? Or would the ending of the Union expose the country to growing hardship at a time of economic uncertainty?

Professor Gavin McCrone brings more than 40 years' experience to bear on these crucial issues. As an academic and, for many years, a senior civil servant, he has been at the heart of economic planning in Scotland – most significantly as Chief Economic Adviser to the Scottish Office from 1970 to 1992 – for much of his career.

He approaches the subject from an objective standpoint, examining each aspect with a strong command of statistics and a dispassionate assessment of their merits. More importantly, perhaps, he comes unswayed by bias. On the one hand, he has advised successive United Kingdom governments on economic policy – a background synonymous with the constitutional status quo. On the other hand, as a senior civil servant in 1974, he compiled a report for Ministers on whether North Sea oil revenues would allow an independent Scotland to manage financially. He concluded that not only they would but also they had the capacity to transform the country's fortunes. His paper remained confidential at the time but, if it had been publicly available, the course of Scottish politics might have been very different.

So neither side can afford to ignore Professor McCrone's analysis. He is, in journalistic terms, 'a reliable source'. More than that, he has the great merit of clarity. He examines each aspect of the independence debate with a combination of straightforward analysis and simply expressed conclusions, providing the bare minimum of statistics, set out in a helpfully comprehensible style.

He addresses head on the questions that most trouble voters – whether floating or not. How wealthy a nation is Scotland? How dependent would it be on oil revenues? Would independence allow the country sufficient flexibility on taxation to bolster its economy? Could it afford to fund the welfare state on which it has grown to depend? Would it gain rapid entry to the EU and, if so, would it have to join the euro? What are the implications of adopting the pound as its currency? Could an independent Scotland have weathered the collapse of its once powerful banks? How viable is its energy policy? Is North Sea oil the key that would unlock its potential, or is it a diminishing and unreliable asset?

Professor McCrone addresses, too, issues that directly affect the personal finances of individual citizens – mortgages, personal borrowing and pensions, all of which could be materially affected were Scotland to become independent. Hitherto, these have been the preserve of Westminster. By tracing the recent history of UK government policy, and its likely development in future years, he places SNP proposals, as set out in its White Paper, into the wider context of British legislation.

Finally, he examines the process of negotiation which

would inevitably follow a vote for separation. It would, he predicts, be 'a major upheaval with uncertain consequences'. And while, with good will on both sides, it could be navigated, no one should underestimate the complexity of what might lie ahead.

In addition to these critical issues, Professor McCrone examines the case for other options facing the nation: differing forms of devolution such as the proposals contained in the current Scotland Act; the so-called Devo-Max plan for full-scale fiscal independence; and its less extreme version, Devo-Plus. He questions the assumptions behind each, making the important point that they would all, in different ways, impinge on other areas of the United Kingdom – not always to beneficial effect – and goes on to develop his own favoured alternative.

The backcloth to these arguments is a decision which will confront every person of voting age living in Scotland. It is a more fundamental one than any they have voted on before. Unlike a general election, where the choice, however far-reaching, can be changed in five years' time, this one is irreversible. If Scotland does, indeed, secede from the United Kingdom to form an independent state, it cannot then decide to rejoin if the outcome is not to its liking. Equally, if the decision is to remain part of the United Kingdom, then that too is one that will endure for many years – 'at least for a generation', in the words of the First Minister, Alex Salmond; and, if any attempt were made to revisit it more frequently than that, it would, in all likelihood, be strongly resisted by the other countries of the UK because it would be destabilising for all of them.

It is therefore important that the implications of this critical choice are fully understood by those who will make it. While many people will rest their decision on personal or emotional grounds, opting perhaps to stay within the

United Kingdom because of family connections or historical legacy, others will feel equally strongly that it is precisely
this history that urges them towards the re-establishment of
an independent Scottish nation.

Whatever the reasons influencing their vote, it is important that everyone who takes part in the referendum has a
clear understanding of the implications for Scotland and the
rest of the United Kingdom. They need answers to the questions that have arisen on the way towards the final decision
and clear guidance on how best these can be answered. This
book provides the road map that should be the essential
companion for all those charged with deciding the future
direction of their country.

Magnus Linklater
January 2014

Preface to the Second Edition

The first edition of this book was published in August 2013. It had sold out by the end of the year. In the meantime, the Scottish Government's white paper had been published, as had much else, including the UK Government's Scotland Analysis series of papers. My own thinking had also evolved, as I thought further about the issues in this very important matter. In this second edition, I have therefore added material to most of the chapters of the first edition and also included a chapter on pensions and mortgages, which I subsequently felt I should have covered in the first edition. The conclusions are mostly the same but are considerably expanded.

I would like to repeat my thanks to Magnus Linklater for his excellent Foreword, to all those who read drafts of the chapters in the first edition and on whose comments I still rely. I would also like to thank Owen Kelly for a valuable discussion about Scotland's financial sector and all those at Birlinn with whom I have enjoyed working for the book's publication. But the opinions expressed in this book and the accuracy of the facts quoted are my responsibility alone.

Gavin McCrone
January 2014

Preface

In 1707 when the members of the Scottish and English Parliaments passed the Act of Union, parliaments were very far from being representative of the people. But, in 2014, it will be for every person of voting age living in Scotland to decide on their country's constitutional future.

There are many Scots living in other parts of the United Kingdom or abroad who have views on this matter and feel they should have been able to vote. But, apart from the major complications that would introduce, I agree with the view taken by the Scottish and UK Governments that it is right for people living in Scotland to be the ones taking the decision. It is they who will live with the consequences of that decision, whatever it may be.

I have no doubt that Scotland could prosper either as an independent country or if it chooses to remain part of the United Kingdom. But the consequences will be substantial whichever way the decision goes. So long as the issues are properly understood – or at least as well understood as the available information allows – there should be no complaint with the decision. This book weighs up the economic issues – it does not attempt to deal with other important issues, such as defence. It is in the belief that many economic aspects of the decision are not well understood, because people lack the information that they need, that I have written this book.

I have never been a member of a political party and I

am beholden to no person or group. I have tried to be as objective as possible in setting out the issues. I realise that this will not satisfy everyone. There will inevitably be those who will disagree with some of the judgements I make. But, if so, I hope that the arguments can be assessed on their merits rather than on the basis of preconceived ideas. In the following pages, there will be criticism of arguments put forward by the present Scottish Government, but there will also be plenty of criticism of what Westminster governments have said and done.

As I write, the independence debate is constantly developing. Scarcely a day goes by without either some change in government policy, a fresh set of statistics, the publication of a report on the subject or just comment in the press. Other books are being published or are planned. I should make it clear therefore that I have not been able to offer an opinion or comment on anything that was published after this book went to press.

I am grateful to Jeremy Peat, Professor David Bell and Sir David Edward, who have each read chapters, and to my son, Angus, who has read much of the book. All have offered valuable comments. Any errors or omissions that remain, however, are my responsibility alone. I am also grateful to my wife, who has uncomplainingly tolerated the many hours I have spent absenting myself from other activities to be in my study writing this book.

Gavin McCrone
March 2013

1

How Well Off Are We?

Economic arguments have formed a large part of the SNP's case for independence, ever since the growth in support for their party in the late 1960s, and these arguments also form an important part of the Scottish Government's recent white paper on independence.[1] For an independence movement this is unusual, although it appears now also to be a factor in Catalonia. Most commonly, when countries split to form independent states, it is because of differences in culture or serious grievances about the way they have been treated. Whatever the economic consequences, they take the view that they simply do not want any longer to be part of the larger state with which they have been associated. There have been numerous examples – the break-up of the Soviet Union, the collapse of Yugoslavia, and even the independence of what then became the Irish Free State and is now the Irish Republic. In this latter case, although the economic condition of Ireland within the UK during much of the previous century and right up to the First World War certainly gave grounds for serious grievance, even there, as with the other countries, little if any detailed argument about the economic consequences of independence or the policies that a separate state might pursue took place. Indeed, what really seems to have brought the issue to a head in Ireland was not so much its economy as the savage and ill-judged reaction of the UK Government to the 1916 uprising in Dublin, which resulted in many of the leaders being executed.

Scotland has its own distinct culture and history. Moreover, during my lifetime I have witnessed the development of a growing awareness of Scotland's separate identity and the confidence that goes with that. Nevertheless, it is not so difficult to understand why the argument about the economy features as much as it does in the Scottish context. Scotland had its industrial revolution early and, during those years, the economy grew rapidly. But this early success left a legacy of problems that was to dominate the economy for much of the 20th century, as it did also in the north of England and South Wales, when the traditional industries of coal, steel, textiles and shipbuilding, together with associated engineering, went into decline. These industries also declined across much of Europe. But they had been very heavily concentrated on the Clyde and in the west of Scotland, where their achievement and the skills that went with them had been a source of pride. Their success resulted in the rapid growth of Glasgow, which was called 'the Second City of the Empire'. It is therefore no surprise that their decline in the 1960s and 1970s, however inevitable, made people feel that the industrial heart was being torn out of Scotland.

While, in the post-war decades, unemployment remained low by present day or pre-war standards, it was frequently twice the rate for the UK and net emigration was extremely high, amounting over the decades of the 1950s and 1960s to a total of 609,000. Approximately half of this was to the rest of the UK and half overseas. This was equivalent to 30 per cent more than the whole population of Edinburgh.[2] There were serious problems of deprivation in some of the industrial areas, notably in the west of Scotland – a problem that persists to this day. Scotland was, of course, not the only part of the UK suffering these problems. But they gave rise to a feeling in Scotland that the country's economy was not doing as well as it should and that the UK Government in London was not doing enough.

The UK Government, through its regional development policy, especially during the 1960s and 1970s when this policy was at its height with substantial funds devoted to it, attempted to deal with this problem. In addition to substantial grants available to encourage industrial investment in areas of high unemployment, the Highlands and Islands Development Board (HIDB) was set up in 1965 and the Scottish Development Agency (SDA) in 1975. Considerable success was achieved through the introduction of new industries, most notably, but by no means exclusively, electronics. Indeed, Scotland was the most successful part of the UK in attracting inward investment from overseas and, after Ireland, one of the most successful in Europe. But this did not eliminate the problem and the success with investment in the electronics industry received a severe setback after 2000, when the industry encountered a recession and much of the new investment went to countries with lower labour costs. What had been achieved was not always recognised and the details of successive regional development policies were largely lost on the general public. After the 1979 election, the new Conservative Government's philosophy was against intervention and in favour of giving full rein to market forces. Assistance through regional policy was scaled down, though it still continues, as do SDA and HIDB. But both of these agencies were significantly modified in the early 1990s and renamed Scottish Enterprise and Highlands and Islands Enterprise. Their scope and remit were again changed by the SNP Government after its election in 2007.

The election of 1979 was followed by a period of severe economic difficulty in Scotland, as it was also in many parts of England, especially in the north. The tight monetary policies followed by the government resulted in the closure of many industrial firms, not only those in the older heavy industries of shipbuilding, steel, coal and heavy engineering but also some inward investment companies, the motor industry at Bathgate and Linwood, the aluminium smelter at Invergordon, and many new businesses that had set up in Scotland. It was at this time that Scotland lost much of its manufacturing industry.

It was ironic that, as North Sea oil production began to flow in substantial quantities, it adversely affected much of Scotland's existing manufacturing through strengthening the UK's balance of payments and pushing up the exchange rate for the pound, so that many businesses became uncompetitive. This is when what should be a boon can become a curse; indeed, it is sometimes called the 'resource curse': one sector of the economy is so strong that it pushes up the exchange rate to the point where it forces a decline in other parts of the economy. In these years, the decline of existing industry appeared to outweigh the very welcome benefits to companies that took advantage of the opportunities available from oil-related activity. I thought at the time that policies were needed to try to counter this adverse effect because, even if much of this was inevitable, it resulted in high unemployment and great distress. The result was that the unemployment rate in Scotland peaked at just under 14 per cent in 1986 – much higher even than in the recent severe recession.[3]

The sense of grievance stemming from the difficulties in the economy in past decades has therefore been a major factor in the growth of support for independence, even if now Scotland's performance relative to the rest of the United Kingdom is significantly improved. Some people felt that Scotland's economic performance, as part of the UK, was below its potential and started to question whether it might do better on its own.

This feeling received a major boost when North Sea oil and gas were discovered in the 1970s. The vast bulk of the oil discoveries (though not the gas) were off the Scottish coast and, under international rules, would have been in Scotland's offshore territory were it an independent state. The importance of this seemed at first to be underestimated by the UK Government and it was some time before appropriate policies to give benefit to the state were put in place but, once this was done, the revenues from taxation were very large indeed and of major benefit to the UK Exchequer. No longer did it seem so persuasive to the general public to argue that Scots would be worse off if their country became independent. It was no surprise therefore that support for independence grew.

How Wealthy Is Scotland?

Scotland's relative economic position within the UK is now enormously better than it was in the early 1970s. The strength of an economy is assessed by using statistics that measure the total of goods and services produced. Two measures are widely used – gross domestic product (GDP) and gross value added (GVA). The difference between the two is not important so long as comparisons are consistent.* Scotland's gross value added (GVA) per head, at 98.6 per cent of the UK average in 2011, was exceeded only by London and the South East of England (Table 1). (This is without the inclusion in any part of the UK of oil and gas output from the North Sea.) At a lower level of aggregation,

---

* GDP relates to output, including sales taxes but not any subsidies, whereas GVA is output excluding indirect taxes but including any subsidies. As indirect taxes are more important than subsidies, GDP figures for Scotland are somewhat higher than GVA. Official statistics now most frequently use GVA whereas, in earlier years, only GDP was available. The reader may find this confusing – some of the comparisons are made in GDP and some in GVA, but that is how they are published by the government statisticians.

the north east of Scotland is now one of the most prosperous parts of the UK, with a GVA per head of 144 per cent of the UK average, second only to Inner London. This compares with the situation in the late 1950s and 1960s, when Scotland's GDP per head was around 10 per cent below the UK average and in some years even lower, making it one of the poorest parts of the UK.[4] In contrast, Wales and the Northern Region of England both seem to have fallen somewhat further behind over the same period, with GVA per head 75.2 per cent and 75.9 per cent of the UK average respectively.

Net migration is now into, rather than out of, Scotland and unemployment at the latest count was fractionally below the UK average.[5] This turnaround is partly a consequence of the 1960s and 1970s regional policies, including the work of Scottish Enterprise and Highlands and Islands Enterprise, but also the remarkable growth in Scotland of the financial services sector and of employment across a range of industries associated with the development of North Sea oil and gas, especially in the North East. In addition, the decline of the older industries has now reduced them to a size where they are no longer such a drag on the performance of the economy.

Scotland is therefore quite a wealthy country, whether compared with the rest of the United Kingdom or internationally, because the United Kingdom itself is one of the wealthier countries in Europe and indeed the world. In the Scottish Government's white paper, Scotland is put at eighth wealthiest.[6] This conclusion is arrived at by adding to Scotland's GDP a Scottish geographical share of the output of the North Sea. This increases Scottish GDP by some 21 per cent[7] and results in Scotland's GDP per head being exceeded in Europe only by Luxembourg, Norway, Switzerland and Monaco.

Table 1

Gross Value Added in 2011 by Country and Region

	GVA per head Index UK = 100	Growth in total GVA since 2010 %	Share of UK total GVA %
United Kingdom	100.0	2.4	100.0
England	102.3	2.3	83.9
North East	75.9	1.5	3.1
North West	85.1	1.9	9.2
Yorkshire and Humber	81.6	1.9	6.8
East Midlands	86.6	2.1	6.1
West Midlands	83.8	2.0	7.1
East of England	92.7	2.9	8.5
London	170.7	2.1	21.1
South East	107.2	3.1	14.3
South West	91.5	2.3	7.6
Scotland	98.6	1.9	8.1
Wales	75.2	2.2	3.5
Northern Ireland	79.2	2.5	2.2

Source: Office of National Statistics, December 2012

However, this should not be accepted without qualification. In the first place, it uses Scotland's share of the North Sea as estimated by Professor Alex Kemp of Aberdeen University, which would give Scotland about 90 per cent of the output and tax revenue.[8] The whole of the UK's offshore area has hitherto been treated for statistical purposes as a separate area and without any divisions. Kemp's estimate is derived by applying the international rules for division of offshore territory between states. It is the best estimate one can get but, as he himself points out, it is not something that is agreed by the rest of the United Kingdom. Negotiations would therefore be needed, as they frequently are between countries, and that may not prove such a simple matter.

Secondly, GDP from oil and gas includes the profits of the oil companies and the income of those working off-shore. Company profits will be distributed to sharehold-ers, the majority of whom are not resident in Scotland, and some of those working offshore also come from other parts of the UK. All of that would be taken account of were we to have estimates of Gross *National* Product (GNP) or Gross *National* Income (GNI), where income paid abroad and in-come received from abroad are both calculated to give a net figure, but no allowance for this is made in GDP. Unfortu-nately, GNP and GNI are much more difficult to estimate and although the Scottish Government has published some estimates that show Scottish GNI some 5 per cent lower than GDP, this work is still at the development stage.[9] The truth of the matter is that Scotland's GDP would, indeed, be some 21 per cent higher, if the output of the North Sea were included, but, leaving aside tax revenue, which is dealt with in the next part of this chapter, it would not make much dif-ference to the living standards of people in Scotland.

Nevertheless, the argument for independence on eco-nomic grounds is still made. Scotland's growth is compared unfavourably with other countries of similar size, many of which have quite different economic circumstances. It is also compared unfavourably with the UK, where growth of output (as measured by GDP or GVA) has been faster than in Scotland over a long period; but this ignores the fact that it is not the growth of output in aggregate but output per head that is a guide to the well-being of the population. In-ward migration has been much higher in the south of Eng-land than in Scotland and it is therefore not surprising that output in aggregate has risen faster for the UK as a whole than for Scotland. But, at the same time, the gap in output per head has narrowed so that in Scotland it is now almost equal to the UK average, showing that Scotland's position has improved when compared with the UK as a whole.

Does Scotland Pay its Way?

Taxes across the United Kingdom, apart from those that are the responsibility of local authorities, are collected by HM Revenue and Customs on behalf of the Treasury. Tax rates, apart from Council Tax and Business Rates, are the same across all countries and regions of the UK, although this may change when, under the recent Scotland Act, the Scottish Government becomes responsible for part of Income Tax. The amount of revenue raised in the various parts of the UK therefore depends mainly on their respective wealth and level of incomes. Public expenditure, on the other hand, is disbursed without any regard for wealth, incomes or tax revenue of a particular part of the UK but with the aim of giving a broadly comparable level of public service. This ought to be related in some way to need and, in the case of spending programmes such as social protection that are UK-wide, this will be the case.

Under this system, there is no need to take account of how far revenue raised in any part of the UK covers the public expenditure in that country or region, since the budget is framed for the UK as a whole. It is not easy, therefore, to establish for which regions or countries expenditure is higher than the revenue raised and for which it is lower. Although there have been a number of academic studies that have given estimates, until recently there were no official estimates except for Scotland. The Silk Commission on devolution in Wales and the Northern Ireland Executive have, however, now produced figures for their territories and both show much larger fiscal deficits than for Scotland.[10] In Wales, public expenditure per head, though higher than the UK average, is not as high as for Scotland but, reflecting the lower GDP per head, tax revenue is much lower; and, for Northern Ireland, expenditure per head is higher than for Scotland, while revenue per head, as for Wales, is lower. No official estimates have been published for English regions, except for identifiable public expenditure. These show that the northern region of England also had public expenditure per head above the UK average and, since its GDP per head was similar to that of Wales, I would expect it also to have a substantial fiscal deficit.

The Scottish Office and, following devolution, the Scottish Government have published annual estimates of government expenditure and revenue since 1991, with figures that go back to 1986. It is far from a straightforward task. While the Treasury publishes figures for 'identifiable expenditure' by country and region, this cannot include those items such as defence, foreign embassies and interest on the National Debt for which there is no breakdown. A share of these items can only be allocated using some ratio such as population. The revenue side is even more difficult. Many people living in Scotland and companies operating in Scotland are not taxed in Scotland but in some other part of the UK. The revenue which relates to Scotland is derived from information collected by HM Revenue and Customs, but has to be estimated. The resulting figures have been criticised, especially by the SNP in the early years. However they have been much improved, are now the responsibility of the SNP Government and give as clear a picture of Scotland's present budgetary position as can be obtained.

What they show is that taxation revenue from Scotland is approximately equal to its population share of the UK. This is not surprising, given that Scotland's GDP per head is only very slightly below the UK average. But public expenditure per head is over 10 per cent above the average for the UK (see Table 2).[11] It has been above the UK average for many years, certainly going back to the 1960s and, according to my calculations, even earlier.[12] In the 1960s, there was a deliberate decision by the then Conservative Government to increase public expenditure in Scotland and in the north-east of England, because of their difficult economic circumstances and need for development.[13] The extent to which Scotland's public expenditure per head has been above the UK average seems to have narrowed over the years, from about 20 per cent above in the 1990s to 15 per cent above in the mid-2000s and 10 per cent above in the latest year. But comparisons are difficult because improvements have been made in the methodology. In earlier years, the comparison was only based on 'identifiable' expenditure but, in recent years, the estimates have included a population share of defence, national debt interest and international services. This larger denominator narrows the gap and makes it difficult to get a continuous series of figures on a consistent basis. Using the Scottish Government's figures for identifiable expenditure only, the gap will still appear to be of the order of 14 per cent.[14]

Table 2

*Total Public Expenditure Per Capita – Scotland and UK
2007–08 to 2011–12*

	2007–08	2008–09	2009–10	2010–11	2011–12
Scotland (£)	10,786	11,302	11,829	12,133	12,134
UK (£)	9,497	10,184	10,764	11,008	10,937
Difference	1,289	1,118	1,065	1,125	1,197
Relative UK=100	*113.6*	*110.0*	*109.9*	*110.2*	*110.9*

Source: Government Expenditure and Revenue Scotland 2011–12, *March 2013*

Before 1979, Scotland's share of public expenditure was determined as a result of annual discussions between the Secretary of State for Scotland and the Chief Secretary to the Treasury. But, since 1979, it has mainly been determined by the Barnett formula and comes in the form of a block grant. The workings of this formula are obscure to most people. But in fact the Barnett formula is quite simple. It is no more than the application of Scotland's population ratio to that of England to determine any change in public expenditure that Scotland receives when public expenditure increases or decreases in England. As such it was thought by many people, myself included, that it would result in a gradual narrowing of the gap between public expenditure per head in Scotland and the UK average. This has been referred to as the Barnett squeeze.

In the event, this has not happened as rapidly as expected. This is due to several factors. First, the formula is only applied to the annual change in public expenditure and this is quite small when compared with the inherited amount from previous years. The formula does not adjust the inherited amount at all, even if there were a decline in the Scottish population. Second, it relates only to the part of public spending controlled by the Scottish Government and not even to all of that, since expenditure on agriculture is separately determined. The biggest single component of public expenditure in Scotland is social protection, which is the responsibility of the UK Government and is not subject to the formula at all. This exceeds spending on health and education combined, the two largest programmes funded by the Scottish Government. Third, the formula has, on occasion, been bypassed if there seemed a pressing need to do so – for example, if there was a national negotiation on wages in some sector of public service such as the NHS.

The upshot is that Scottish public expenditure per head, as Table 2 shows, was still £1,197 per head higher than the UK average in 2011–12.[15] Not only does this result in expenditure being substantially higher than tax revenue (excluding tax revenue from the North Sea) but it is also a source of periodic and growing complaint in England, where it is taken to mean that Scotland is subsidised by the UK. Only if public expenditure in the various parts of the UK was seen to be clearly related to need could it be properly defended against such complaints. But no needs assessment has been carried out since a Treasury study in the late 1970s. This was done then in preparation for the devolution scheme in the 1970s, which was never implemented. It appeared to show that, at the time, Scottish public expenditure was indeed higher than an assessment of need would justify, when compared with what is spent in other parts of the UK. Scotland obviously does have special needs – particularly the higher costs associated with providing services in remote communities with a scattered population, and the poor health record and deprivation in some urban areas, especially in the west of Scotland. But incomes in Scotland are now much closer to the UK average than in the 1970s, when the assessment was done, and, although in the absence of an up-to-date needs assessment no firm conclusion can be drawn, it seems unlikely that it would fully justify the level of public expenditure that Scotland currently receives as compared with other parts of the UK.

The counterpart of the Calman Commission in Scotland, which led to the enhanced powers for the Scottish Government contained in the 2012 Scotland Act, was the Holtham Commission in Wales.[16] Using the formula used for distributing public expenditure in England and applying it to Wales and Scotland, Holtham concluded that Wales, although also receiving public expenditure per head above the UK average, received too small a share of UK public expenditure and Scotland too much. This was largely because Scotland's income per head (as measured by GDP) was much higher than that of Wales, which was well below the UK average.

If this was all there was to this subject, one would have to conclude that the government of an independent Scotland, responsible for all taxation and public expenditure, would find itself with a very substantial budget deficit, amounting to 14.6 per cent of GDP in 2011–12, according to the Scottish Government's own figures in *Government Expenditure and Revenue Scotland 2011–12* (GERS). But that takes no account of the revenue from North Sea oil and gas that would accrue to an independent Scotland. If the revenue from the geographical share that would belong to Scotland as an independent state is included, following Kemp's analysis, this reduces the deficit to 8.1 per cent of GDP in 2010–11 and to 5.0 per cent in 2011–12 – still high, but less than the UK deficit of 7.9 per cent in the same year.

Both of these deficits are, of course, unsustainable. They are a consequence of the financial crash of 2008 and the recession that followed. This caused tax revenue to fall sharply and expenditure on benefits to rise as unemployment increased. The austerity measures imposed by the UK Government are intended to get the UK deficit down, but the economy has shrunk, partly as a consequence of the austerity, and economic growth has been badly affected, so that the targets for reducing the deficit have had to be repeatedly extended. In his Autumn Statement of 2013, however, the Chancellor showed that economic growth had at last improved and, although public debt was still rising, he forecast a steady reduction in the deficit and even a modest surplus by 2018–19. Such forecasts are of course subject to constant revision, but it is welcome news that the recovery seems to be gaining ground.

How realistic is the Scottish figure for the deficit of 5.0 per cent in 2011–12? It is of course hypothetical since, as part of the UK, Scotland does not have to balance its public revenue and expenditure. The Scottish Government's white paper says it shows that Scotland is in a stronger financial position than the UK.[17] Is that really so? A number of qualifications have to be made.

In the first place, it is still a deficit, and a deficit that is unsustainable. If Scotland had to balance its own budget, measures would be required to reduce it. Second, it is dependent on the geographical share of North Sea revenues accruing to Scotland. A more detailed discussion of the importance of North Sea oil will be found in Chapter 7. Suffice it to say here that the Scottish Government's assumptions about the North Sea, as explained earlier, use the geographical share of the North Sea based on the median line as estimated by Professor Alex Kemp but, as he himself said in evidence to the House of Commons Committee on Energy and Climate Change, the median line would be taken as the starting point and negotiations would be necessary.[18] All this would take time and could involve arbitration.

Whatever the outcome of such negotiations, the revenues from the North Sea are of course substantial, but they are also very volatile, depending on the output from the North Sea in any one year, on the price of oil and on the profits made by the oil companies. They have varied from about £1 billion a year to over £12 billion. At their peak in the early 1980s, they were very large indeed, whereas, from the mid-1980s, when the price fell sharply, they were much reduced and, in the early 1990s, would have been insufficient, had they accrued to Scotland, to cover the fiscal deficit. Even over the last three years they have shown great volatility: £12.9 billion in 2008–09, falling to £6.5 billion in 2009–10, rising again to £8.8 billion in 2010–11, then £11.3 billion in 2011–12, and £6.5 billion in 2012–13.

For the future, the Office for Budget Responsibility forecasts the Scottish share in oil and gas revenues falling to around £4 billion by 2015–16, although this has been contested by the Scottish Government, which claims that this is less than the oil companies themselves are predicting. The fact is that nobody really knows and one can only speculate. Oil production peaked in 1999 and it is now well below its peak level. It may stabilise or even rise slightly for a while, but the expected long-run trend is for a gradual decline. Revenue depends of course not just on output but also on the price, and prices have proved very volatile. For the future, the outlook for prices is particularly uncertain – on the one hand, the rapid development of countries such as China and India may push prices up but, on the other, the exploitation of shale gas, which is now a major factor in the United States and may become one in Europe, could keep them down. Even if, as many expect, prices stay high, profitability may fall as companies exploit more marginal and less profitable fields and the costs mount of removing structures from fields that have ceased production. These various factors are discussed in Chapter 7.

It is the stated policy of the present Scottish Government that, when conditions allow, the North Sea revenues, or at least a proportion of them, would be paid into a special fund.[19] In this, they are influenced by the example of Norway, which set up such a fund in 1990. This, too, is discussed in Chapter 7. Given the likely variability in revenue from taxation on oil and gas, putting the proceeds into a special fund would mean that its volatility would not affect the annual budget. It also makes sense because using oil revenues to finance ordinary public expenditure amounts to running down a capital asset to finance current spending.

But, while paying the North Sea revenues into such a fund would be very desirable, the government of an independent Scotland could not do without this revenue to finance its budget, so long as the balance between expenditure and revenue remained as it is now. Setting North Sea revenue aside for a special fund would therefore only mean that even more draconian steps would have to be taken to eliminate the budget deficit. In the longer run, the situation may be different – one would hope so – but this would require quite a transformation in the Scottish economy, either by reducing the need for such a high level of public expenditure or somehow increasing other tax receipts through economic growth.

There is a further uncertainty over the balance in what would become the budget of an independent Scotland. The figures in *Government Expenditure and Revenue Scotland 2011–2012* allocate the UK's interest payments on the National Debt on a per capita basis. For an independent Scotland, the National Debt would first have to be split with the rest of the UK. It could be done on a per capita basis, but this might be resisted by the UK Government on the grounds that, as Scotland's GDP was increased by the addition of output from the North Sea, it would be reasonable to allocate the National Debt by the share of GDP. That would make it some 21 per cent higher than a per capita allocation. It would appear that the Scottish Government accepts a per capita basis for attributing Scotland's share of the National Debt, although it has also argued for a historical share, using figures since 1980. This would result in a lower share because it includes the period of very high oil revenues, especially the first half of the 1980s. But if a historical basis is used for attributing Scotland's share, why go back only to 1980? This is when the oil revenues started on a large scale; going back further would go into years when there was a significant deficit. The likelihood, therefore, is that a per capita share would form the basis for negotiation.

Jim and Margaret Cuthbert, in an interesting paper for the Jimmy Reid Foundation, have made an important point about government debt.[20] As a result of the Bank of England's programme of quantitative easing, whereby the Bank bought government bonds as a means of injecting money into the economy to reduce the severity of the recession, it now holds £375 billion, or just over 30 per cent of the total UK public sector debt. Not only that, but the interest it receives on this debt is returned to the government. In effect, therefore, this large amount of debt is costing the government nothing. What will eventually happen to it? In theory it should be sold on the market when conditions improve. But any attempt to sell it in the foreseeable future would cause the price of these bonds to fall, interest on them to rise and a substantial amount of money to be withdrawn from the economy. This could certainly choke the recovery in the economy and it seems unlikely to happen unless there is a real danger of inflation, requiring a cut-back in money supply. It may be that the bonds will simply sit with the Bank of England indefinitely. The Cuthberts raise the possibility that they may eventually just be written off. If these bonds were excluded, UK public sector net debt would be reduced from the present 77 per cent of GDP to about 53 per cent, a much more reasonable sum. The government has not defaulted on repayment of debt since the reign of Charles II, a record of which it is proud. The question, therefore, arises whether a failure to pay off this debt held by the Bank, effectively the government repaying itself, could be regarded as a default!

For an independent Scotland, the important point about this is that if it agreed to take an appropriate share of the total debt, some 30 per cent of that could be bonds that were in effect costless to the UK government because the Bank of England was returning the interest payments. And if at some time in the future a decision was taken to write off this 30 per cent, it should be written off for Scotland's share too. This is not a matter that is widely understood and to many people it will seem a technical question. But it is very important and could make a significant difference to the government budget of an independent Scotland.

Without taking account of this, the GERS estimate for interest on the national debt in 2011–12 was £4,072 million, assuming a population share. There would be uncertainty over the rate of interest that a Scottish government would have to pay, whatever level of debt it took on. It probably would not be, as assumed in GERS, the same rate of interest as for the UK. Theoretically, the rate of interest on Scottish debt might be either higher or lower than for the rest of the UK. But the rate on UK debt is currently at a historic low and there must be doubt over whether this would be matched for Scottish debt, unless agreement was reached to issue common sterling bonds for both countries. That seems unlikely; it would certainly require stringent conditions on fiscal policy to be met that satisfied both countries. Otherwise, as a newly independent country, Scotland would have to establish its credibility as a borrower, with not only the rating agencies but also potential lenders. Even a 1 per cent addition to the rate of interest paid on new borrowing would significantly increase the cost to Scotland. A number of factors are important here – not least whether or not Scotland has its own currency and whether, if it continues to use sterling, there is a credible lender of last resort. There is also a question over how Scotland would assume its share of the debt. Would Scotland simply become indebted to the UK Government until an appropriate share of the debt had been paid off, or would Scotland have to raise new debt immediately after independence to pay off its share? How this is done could have a substantial effect on the interest cost to be paid.[21] The consequence of all these reservations is that it would be unwise to assume, in the event of Scotland becoming independent, that its deficit would actually turn out to be as it is given in the GERS estimate. It could possibly be lower, but it much more likely to be higher.

A study published by the independent Institute for Fiscal Studies (IFS) in the autumn of 2013, which attracted attention in the press, argues that, while both Scotland and the UK face a problem of continuing deficits that will lead to rising National Debt for some years yet, the outlook for Scotland is much more difficult than for the UK as a whole.[22] This is for two reasons: first, because the oil and gas revenues that would be so important to Scotland's fiscal position are forecast to decline; and second, because Scotland's population is expected to age more rapidly. Most developed countries face pressure on public finances from increases in longevity and lack of growth in the size of the working population, but Scotland's position is worse than the UK's, mainly because immigration has been a larger element in the population south of the border, where it has boosted the share of the population of working age.

The IFS projection shows that by 2017–18 the deficit for the UK between spending and revenues will have fallen to 2.2 per cent as a result of present policies, but for Scotland it will still be 4.3 per cent and would rise further thereafter unless additional steps are taken to curb it. This is a depressing conclusion, but it is simply the result of the arithmetic based on the IFS assumptions for decline in revenue from the North Sea coupled with an ageing population. Only a faster growth in population of working age, resulting most probably from greater immigration than in the past, coupled with a sharply increased growth in the economy's output, whether from the North Sea or the rest of the economy, would be capable of producing a different result.

It would be wrong to leave this subject, however, without considering what might happen in future under the present arrangements, whether or not there is an enhanced degree of devolution. Quite apart from the view expressed by the Holtham Commission, there has been an increasingly strong view in England that, under the Barnett formula arrangements, Scotland receives a more generous share of public expenditure than is justified. Sooner or later this must be likely to lead to some action by a future UK Government. This is counterbalanced by a fear in Scotland that, since the Barnett formula is only a population ratio, it will eventually result in the squeeze that was earlier expected. As already explained, it is impossible to tell whether the present level of public expenditure, and in particular the extent to which it is above the UK average, is justified in the absence of a proper needs assessment.

So far, pressure to address this issue has been ignored, and David Cameron has said as recently as December 2013 that his government has no plans to alter the formula. But a time may well come when this line can no longer be sustained and a revised system is introduced that allocates expenditure more closely in relation to need. If that happens, it would be important that it should be based on a full needs assessment across all the regions and countries of the UK and is carried out by an independent body, acceptable both to the three devolved administrations and to the government of the UK. Scotland would very probably then find itself required to reduce its public spending. I have always taken the view that, sooner or later, this would be inevitable, but that the adjustment should be planned over a long period and at a time when the economy was buoyant. It would clearly be painful and would have major political consequences if attempted in circumstances such as the present.

Actually, since Scotland's population is only about 8.4 per cent of the total population of the UK, a redistribution of spending between the four countries of the UK to accord with a needs assessment would make little difference to England, where it would scarcely be noticed by the average voter. But that would certainly not be the case in Scotland. It may be, therefore, that the present arrangements will endure for a considerable time, simply because the UK Government might not think it worth the hassle of making a change or of incurring political problems in Scotland, when the constitutional issue is in the minds of the electorate.

What this means, however, is that, whether Scotland remains part of the UK under any scheme of devolution or becomes independent, there is likely to be pressure on its level of public spending. Independence would involve uncertainty both over the level and volatility of oil and gas revenues, for which the prudent policy would suggest that relying on them to balance the budget should be avoided and a part of them at least should be paid into a special fund. Remaining a devolved part of the UK, on the other hand, is likely to mean that eventually the level of expenditure will have to be justified through a needs assessment. The crucial difference is that, as an independent state, Scotland would be entirely responsible for its budget from the time that it became independent and would have to live within its means. But, as part of a larger state, the revenue and expenditure of the individual countries and regions that form the UK would not need to balance. With broadly comparable taxes, the richer areas would contribute more than those that were poorer and expenditure would not be related to the revenue of a particular country or region but to what is required to provide a comparable level of public services.

2

Devo-Max, Devo-Plus and the Status Quo: Economic Policy with Devolution

The independence debate has seen the publication of several schemes that could have formed the basis of a third option in the 2014 referendum to give greater devolution. Although the polls show those who support independence varying around 30 per cent of the electorate, they also show that a larger percentage would favour remaining in the UK but with greater devolution had that option been available in the referendum.

What might such an option have amounted to? It is worth considering this, even if it is not an option in the referendum, because, in recognition of popular pressure, all three unionist parties are said to be working on options for greater devolution, which may lead to implementation after the referendum. The results of this work are expected in the spring, though it is not clear whether there will be any agreed proposal; indeed, the Better Together campaign has been criticised for having put forward nothing so far. At present, therefore, neither the details nor the implications of a third option are well understood; nor are many people yet fully aware of what the status quo would amount to because the Scotland Act 2012 has not yet taken effect and will take some time to do so. Even the status quo, therefore, does not mean continuing with devolution as it has been since 1999. That is no longer possible.

The Status Quo

If independence is rejected in the referendum and the UK Government brings forward no further proposals to enhance devolution, the Scotland Act 2012 will form the basis of the system of government in Scotland. This will increase the powers of the Scottish Parliament as set out in the UK Government's white paper *Strengthening Scotland's Future*,[1] which closely followed the recommendations of the Calman Commission on Scottish devolution set up by the three unionist parties in the Scottish Parliament.[2]

Much of the Act is concerned with working arrangements between the two governments, but the most important provisions, and those that concern us here, are those that are designed to give greater responsibility to the Scottish Parliament for raising revenue. It has been a major criticism of devolution since 1999 that the Scottish Parliament had responsibility for a large part of public expenditure in Scotland but very little for raising the revenue to finance it. That resulted, it is argued, in insufficient accountability for the spending decisions that Parliament makes. Under the system that has applied since 1999, the only taxes for which there is any responsibility in Scotland are Council Tax and Business Rates. The Act setting up the Parliament gave power to vary the standard rate of Income Tax either up or down by 3 pence in the pound, but this power was never used. As a result, only 14 per cent of expenditure for which responsibility lies in Scotland is financed by taxes set in Scotland.[3]

The principal change is that, in future, the Scottish Parliament will be required to set a Scottish rate of Income Tax each year to replace part of the UK Income Tax. From April 2016, the UK Government will reduce the main UK rates of Income Tax in Scotland by 10 pence. The block grant will be reduced by a similar amount to compensate, leaving the Scottish Parliament to determine what rate of Income Tax to levy, in place of the 10 pence, to finance its expenditure. Responsibility for the structure of tax rates will remain with Westminster but, if changes are made by the UK Parliament to the structure of Income Tax rates, a principle of 'no detriment' will apply. This would result in compensating changes to the block grant to ensure that Scottish Government revenue is not affected.

This power over Income Tax represents a large flow of income – if the Scottish tax rate were 10 pence in the pound, it would raise £4,500 million, or 17 per cent, of the Scottish budget.[4] The Scottish rate of tax will apply to all those defined as Scottish taxpayers. This includes those resident in Scotland and those whose principal connection with the UK is with Scotland.

The Calman Commission found that the cost of applying the Scottish rate of tax to income from savings and distributions would be prohibitive and recommended instead that half of the tax revenue from this income should be assigned to the Scottish Government. The white paper accepts that applying the Scottish rate of tax to income from these sources is impractical but argues that assigning tax revenues does not enhance accountability. For this reason, neither assignment nor power to alter the rates on income from savings and distributions were included in the Act.

However, in addition to a share of Income Tax, the Act gives the Scottish Parliament complete responsibility for stamp duty tax on land and property (but not on documents or stock exchange transactions) and for tax on landfill. The revenue from these two taxes, however, is relatively modest compared with Income Tax. The Calman Commission recommended devolution of two further taxes – the tax on air passengers and that on aggregates. The revenue from them would also have been fairly modest, but they are not included in the Scotland Act 2012; the former is presently being reviewed and the latter is subject to legal challenge in the European Courts. However, the Act also gives the Scottish Government power to levy any new taxes, subject to approval by both the Scottish and UK Parliaments.

The effect of devolving the three taxes in the Scotland Act, together with the responsibility that already exists for Council Tax and Business Rates, is to increase to about 35 per cent the share of budget revenue for which the Scottish Parliament and local authorities would be responsible.[5] The white paper argues that the revenue from these devolved taxes would finance a similar share of the Scottish Government's budget to that of the devolved legislatures in Belgium, Italy, Spain and Australia.

In addition to these tax powers, the Act gives the Scottish Parliament substantial new powers to borrow. Under the arrangements that have applied since 1999, Scottish Ministers have had only limited power to borrow for short-term current spending and this power was never used. In future, because income from taxation is less predictable than from the UK block grant, the new arrangements involve a degree of risk that has not hitherto existed. To allow for temporary shortfalls resulting from this, as well as deviations between forecast revenues and expenditure, Scottish Ministers are to be given power to borrow up to £500 million for cumulative current debt. In addition, they will have power to borrow up to 10 per cent of the capital budget in any one year, with a limit of £2.2 billion on the total stock of borrowing for capital investment.[6]

This regime would reduce the share of public expenditure financed by the block grant to 65 per cent. At present, as Chapter 1 explained, this grant is determined by the Barnett formula and has attracted much criticism, especially in England. But, apart from reducing the share of public expenditure that the formula would finance, there are no proposals to change it.

While these changes in taxation and borrowing will increase the accountability of the Scottish Parliament, they do not do anything to give the Scottish Parliament power and responsibility over macroeconomic policy. Indeed, the white paper explicitly reserves this to Westminster. That does not mean, of course, that the Scottish Government cannot adopt policies that improve the performance of the economy. Ways in which Scotland's economic growth might be improved with the Scottish Government's existing responsibilities are discussed later in this chapter. Suffice it to say here that those who look for some independence in macroeconomic policy must accept that responsibility over demand management through monetary, fiscal and exchange rate policies must inevitably rest with the state and, in Scotland's case, even with devolution, that state is still the UK.

Devo-Max

Devo-Max has never been very clearly defined, but it presumably means almost total fiscal separation of Scotland from the rest of the UK. Contributions would still be required to meet the costs of common services such as the royal family, defence, servicing the national debt and foreign embassies; monetary union with the rest of the UK would continue and foreign exchange reserves would be held for the UK as a whole. Only for this reduced range of functions would the UK Parliament continue to have any responsibility for Scotland. This would, of course, raise questions about whether the existing number of Westminster MPs could be justified. The main feature of such an arrangement, however, is that there would be no social pact. If Scotland were

wealthier than other parts of the UK, it would not be expected to contribute support for them and, if Scotland was
poorer or had some sudden crisis, perhaps through the collapse of a major industry, it could not expect any help from
the rest of the UK. No attempt would be made to equalise
social provision; and welfare benefits, including state pensions, might be at different rates from their equivalents elsewhere in the UK.

It is not easy to find examples of this kind of arrangement in other countries. The Campbell Committee said it
was not aware of any.[7] The case that seems to come nearest
to it is that of the Basque country and Navarra in Spain
and this is referred to by the Scottish Government.[8] The
Basque country has a higher GDP per head than the Spanish average but has a population of only two million, 5 per
cent of the Spanish total. In a recent paper for the David
Hume Institute, César Colino argued that this system has
been profitable for the Basque country because of its relative wealth.[9] Unsurprisingly, it has attractions for the areas
that are richer than the rest of the country but is considered
unjust by the others.

Even here, however, there is not complete fiscal autonomy. In accordance with EU rules, there can be no separate
rate of VAT for an area that forms part of a member state;
and the Spanish state retains responsibilities for social security, justice, defence, foreign affairs, transfers to the EU,
macroeconomic policy and regulation of the financial sector. A contribution for these central services is paid by the
Basque country to the Spanish state. Indeed, even with this
large amount of devolution, 50 per cent of Basque public
expenditure, mainly for state pensions and unemployment
benefits, remains the responsibility of the central government which also raises 40 per cent of the public revenues.[10]
The Basque country, therefore, remains subject to fiscal de-

cisions made by central government, including the policies to reduce the Spanish budget deficit. The Spanish Government has also had to defend its fiscal arrangements for the Basque country against appeals from the European Commission at the European Court of Justice.

Could such a system work in Scotland? As was shown in the last chapter, public spending per head is some 10 per cent above the UK average, while revenues, excluding oil and gas, are no more than equal to the average. So, unless the Scottish Government received a geographical share of oil and gas revenues, there would have to be some sharp cuts in public expenditure. The geographical share of North Sea revenue would approximately cover the higher level of spending at present but, according to the Institute for Fiscal Studies, will not do so in future as oil and gas revenues decline and the Scottish population ages faster than that of the UK as a whole. Apart from this potential problem, Scotland would be fully exposed to the volatility of these revenues from year to year. Moreover, so long as Scotland remained a part of the UK, the rest of the UK might see it as unreasonable to give Scotland so much of the North Sea revenue and might resist any change. At present the offshore area is not divided between different countries in the UK but is treated as a resource for the benefit of the whole state. The UK Government would probably want that to continue.

Under Devo-Max there could still be no separate rate of VAT and there would be problems in devolving welfare and social security (welfare devolution is discussed in Chapter 8). Different rates of state pension or contributory benefits, such as jobseeker's allowance, might be unacceptable within what is still one state. There could be a strong political reaction from any part of the UK that felt it was disadvantaged by the financial arrangements for Scotland. Indeed, it could well be that, rather than accept such an arrangement, the rest of the UK might prefer to let Scotland become an independent state.

Some experts have argued that fiscal independence would encourage the Scottish Government to put a greater emphasis on economic growth, so that its economy performed better. Professors Andrew Hughes Hallett and Drew Scott were subjected to close questioning on this by a committee of the Scottish Parliament in early 2011 after asserting that there was evidence of this from other parts of the world.[11] But the evidence is not very convincing and, in Scotland's case, politicians of all parties share a commitment to try to improve the country's rate of economic growth. If they were aware of measures that would improve the country's performance, they should already be adopting them.

Devo-Plus

Several suggestions have been put forward for giving Scotland more devolution than will be provided by the Scotland Act 2012 but not going as far as Devo-Max. Indeed, there have been so many proposals that many people may find them confusing. The following paragraphs outline and discuss three such schemes from:

- an inter-party group of Liberal Democrat, Labour and Conservative MSPs chaired by Jeremy Purvis and published by Reform Scotland;[12]
- a committee set up by the Liberal Democrats, chaired by Sir Menzies Campbell;[13]
- a report for the Institute of Public Policy Research (IPPR) by Professor Alan Trench.[14]

This last seeks to outline a system that could be applicable to all three devolved administrations in the UK and contains the most comprehensive discussion of what is possible. All of these see major advantages for Scotland in remaining part of the UK but consider that there is a case for additional fiscal powers to make devolution more acceptable. Both the Purvis group and the Campbell Committee would like the Scottish Parliament to be entrenched by legislation, so that it could only be dissolved if it agreed, and the UK Parliament's power to legislate on devolved matters removed. The Campbell Committee would see this as a step towards a proper federal constitution for the UK.

The Purvis group's proposals, which are in three stages, go much further than the others and raise some of the same difficulties as were noted with Devo-Max. All three sets of proposals include complete devolution of Income Tax, but the Campbell Committee would retain the same system of allowances and reliefs throughout the UK and does not consider that taxation from savings and investments could be devolved. It suggests assignment of the revenue instead. Purvis proposes devolution of Corporation Tax by 2020, something the SNP Scottish Government would also like; the Campbell Committee, on the other hand, does not consider it an appropriate tax to devolve; and Trench outlines the substantial difficulties for both companies and tax authorities. He refers to the dangers of companies shifting their profits to the part of the UK with the lowest tax and concludes that it would only be possible if profits were allocated between the constituent countries and regions of the UK on the basis of payroll.

The estimate in the Scottish Government's publication *Government Expenditure and Revenue Scotland* for Corporation Tax revenue is £2,976 million for 2011–12, but, while that relates to activity in Scotland, it is not known how much of it is actually paid in Scotland. Companies will usually pay where their registered office is and for many of the larger companies operating in Scotland that may be in England. No one knows, therefore, how much a Scottish Government would actually receive if the tax were devolved, unless it was agreed to allocate it by payroll, as Trench proposes. This would be an issue even if Scotland was independent. Shifting profits to low tax areas is also a problem internationally and companies such as Google, Amazon and Starbucks have been criticised in consequence.

Only the Purvis group proposes eventual devolution of a geographical share of North Sea revenues. The Campbell Committee argues that the whole of Britain's offshore area should be under a single regime and not divided, while Trench suggests that a population share of the revenues could be allocated to the Scottish Government. None of the three propose devolution of VAT, as different rates of this tax within a single member state are not permitted under EU rules, but Trench suggests that the revenue (apart from the contribution that goes to the EU) could be assigned to the devolved administrations. None of the schemes propose devolving responsibility for national insurance. This accords with their views on welfare expenditure. Although the Purvis group would like the Scottish Government to be given a larger role in welfare, all three accept that the bulk of welfare expenditure, including the state pension, should remain with the UK Government. In the end, taking account also of the other smaller taxes it wishes to see devolved, the Purvis group's proposals would result in almost all of the expenditure of the Scottish Government and local authorities eventually being covered by taxes raised in Scotland. The other two sets of proposals would result in around 55 per cent being financed by taxes raised in Scotland; they would therefore need to be supplemented by a significant but smaller block grant.

Both the Campbell and Trench proposals recognise that the block grant, as determined by the Barnett formula, is no longer acceptable to the whole of the UK and that it should move to a system based on an assessment of need. This would still give Scotland a bigger grant than a straight equalisation of fiscal revenue, such as applies in some federal countries, but the adjustment would be likely to involve a significant cut. The assessment should be carried out for all four countries of the UK and, ideally, for the English regions as well, and it is important that it should be done by an independent body in which all the administrations have confidence.

Assessment of Devo-Plus

How realistic are these proposals? It would certainly be possible to go beyond the changes made in the Scotland Act 2012. The Scottish Parliament could be made responsible for a greater share of Income Tax than the 10 pence envisaged under the Act. The case against this, as the Calman report argues, is that it could be unwise to have the Scottish Government too heavily dependent on one tax, the proceeds of which could be volatile. Moreover, if the UK Government had no locus at all in setting Income Tax in Scotland, it would have to rely on other taxes – particularly VAT – to provide for servicing the UK national debt, for defence and for dealing with emergencies such as arose in recent years to support the banks. All of these taxes are to a varying extent regressive and such expenditure could be substantial, as well as subject to variation, as unexpected needs arise. So if the whole of Income Tax were devolved, it would have major implications for the UK Government's ability to affect the distribution of the tax burden. If it had suddenly to increase tax revenue for some emergency and had no power over Income Tax, recourse to a higher rate of VAT would affect the poorer people in the population more than a rise in Income Tax would have done. The UK Government, in my view, ought to retain a role to enable it to tackle income inequality and much of its ability to deal with this would be lost without responsibility for at least some part of Income Tax. These considerations, therefore, point to some share of Income Tax remaining with the UK Parliament.

The Purvis group envisages the eventual devolution of fuel duty and excise duties, but this is not proposed by the Campbell Committee, and Trench only considers it for duties on alcohol and tobacco. Together these duties amounted to over £4 billion in 2011–12, which could very usefully augment the Scottish Government's responsibility for tax revenue. Devolution of the duties on alcohol and tobacco would also be attractive because of their potential relationship with the Scottish Government's health policy. But Trench shows there would be considerable difficulty because they are levied not at the point of sale but of production or import. Devolution of fuel duties was considered by Calman. The problem there is that they are levied at the point of production, which is the Grangemouth refinery, for most of Scotland. But the Grangemouth refinery also serves the north of England and under EU rules fuel duty rates are required to be set nationally.[15] The Scottish and UK Governments have obtained an EU derogation to enable lower prices to be charged in the Scottish islands, through a cut in duty, because prices there were particularly high, but to get such a derogation for the whole of Scotland would be much more difficult. In view of the size of these revenues, these difficulties are disappointing. The need for a derogation from the EU would, of course, not arise if Scotland were a separate state, but that would not avoid the other problems and would require major changes in how these taxes are collected.

If the issue of accountability is a major concern, as I believe it to be, it would be possible to follow the practice in some other countries and assign the proceeds of VAT (as proposed by Trench) and some of the smaller taxes to the Scottish Parliament but without freedom to alter tax rates. Some people regard tax assignment as pointless if tax rates cannot be altered. But it would tie Scottish public expenditure more closely to the revenue actually generated in Scotland, enable the block grant to be much smaller and perhaps give less scope to taxpayers elsewhere in the UK to complain about unfair funding for Scotland. And, if the Scottish Government was able through its policies to encourage the growth of the economy, it would get the benefit in increased revenue, just as it would get reduced revenue if the economy's growth disappointed. These are not considerations that should be lightly dismissed. Although variation in VAT rates would not be permitted under EU rules, assignment would bring some of the benefits that proponents of Devo-Max argue for.

Corporation Tax is a contentious issue. The SNP Government has made it plain that it would like this tax devolved.[16] The difficulties involved in devolving this tax are considerable, as has already been explained. There are, however, a number of countries – Switzerland is an example – where corporate tax rates are set by the regions (in Switzerland's case, the Cantons). Following the judgment of the European Court of Justice in the Azores case, the EU only permits different rates of Corporation Tax within one member state if the region in which the tax is lower is not subsidised for this purpose by the rest of the state. Otherwise it would be regarded as a state aid and subject to the competition rules on state aids. The Holtham Commission on a funding settlement for Wales has proposed a rebate or a lower rate of tax, based on the proportion of payroll, where levels of GDP are well below the average of the state.[17] That would make it part of regional policy to encourage investment in poorer areas, even if it had to be financed by the region itself. However, since Scotland's GDP per head is very close to the UK average, this would not apply, even if such a scheme were eventually implemented elsewhere in the UK.

In a UK context, I have always regarded devolution of Corporation Tax rates as raising major difficulties. The strongest case is that made for Northern Ireland, where it can be argued there is a competitive disadvantage because the standard rate of Corporation Tax in the neighbouring Irish Republic is only 12.5 per cent. The SNP Government's desire to have control of this tax seems to stem from the Irish Republic's success in using it to attract inward investment, but it has also resulted in companies simply basing their registered offices in Ireland (the so-called 'brass plate effect'). Even in such cases, of course, Ireland has still benefitted from tax on the revenue declared at the registered office.

If Scotland had ambitions to follow this example while still part of the UK, it would help to attract investment to Scotland so long as the difference in tax rates was substantial, but much of this might be at the expense of other parts of the UK and would be particularly resented in Wales, the north of England, or other regions where GDP per head is lower than in Scotland. They would probably make a case for equal treatment to avoid unacceptable distortions. For these reasons, I would expect it to be strongly resisted by the UK Government. Moreover, the Scottish Government already has power over Business Rates, which yield almost £2 billion a year and can be altered as it thinks fit. A lower rate of Corporation Tax would reduce revenue for the Scottish Government, which Trench estimates at a loss of £1.7 billion a year, if it were cut to the Irish Republic's rate. Unless it provided such a stimulus to the economy that it made up for the loss, this would be a problem for the government and, even if there was a significant stimulus, it would take years to make up for the lost revenue.

Oil and gas revenues were proposed for devolution by the Purvis group for the third stage of its scheme. But, as argued already in relation to Devo-Max, so long as Scotland remained part of the UK, there would be no formal need for any division of the offshore area, and I suspect that the UK Government would want to continue to treat it as a resource for the whole UK. I would therefore expect its strong resistance to any change.

A Proposal for Increased Tax Devolution

Table 1 sets out a suggested scheme for increased devolution of taxes that seems to me realistic and would have a chance of being acceptable. It builds on the Devo-Plus proposals of the Campbell Committee and Alan Trench but does not accept all their suggestions. The main difference is that only three-quarters of income tax revenue would be devolved on the grounds that to cope with unexpected demands and emergencies the UK Government should retain some power to levy such a major tax. This introduces a complication, however, because if a Scottish Government wanted to alter the structure of Income Tax, which I think it should have power to do, the UK component would have to be separated and possibly form a separate tax. This would be necessary if the Scottish Government had a different view from the UK Government over which group in society should bear the greatest tax burden. I would assign the revenue of VAT, subject only to the deduction for the required funding for the EU, while accepting that there would be no power to alter rates. This is because I attach importance to making revenue from taxes in Scotland cover as much of public expenditure as practicable. It would also enable the Scottish Government to benefit from any increased revenue as a result of improved economic performance.

Table 1

Scottish Revenue in 2011–12 from Taxes Proposed for Devolution

	£million
Income Tax (three quarters of total)	8,092
VAT (minus EU contribution)	9,269
Insurance premium tax	251
Aggregates levy	52
Landfill tax	97
Stamp duty land tax	275
Air passenger duty	213
Council Tax	1,987
Business Rates	1,933
Total	22,169
Total Scottish government and local authority expenditure	38,624
Taxation revenue as a % of expenditure	57.4

Source: Government Expenditure and Revenue Scotland 2011–12, *March 2013*

Together with the other smaller taxes in the Scotland Act, and the air passenger duty and aggregates levy, which were proposed by Calman but not so far implemented, the revenue from these taxes would cover over half the present expenditure of the Scottish Government and local authorities. The block grant would then be substantially reduced. In order to be capable of robust defence, I consider it unavoidable that the grant that remained would have to be gradually adjusted to accord with a proper needs assessment. Such an assessment, however, should be undertaken by an independent body to ensure that the distribution of expenditure between all the countries and regions of the UK was fair; and moving to it should be in accordance with a timetable agreed by all three devolved administrations and the government of the UK.

My proposed scheme may not go as far as some people might wish but, together with proposals for increased devolution of welfare, outlined in Chapter 8, go as far as I consider practical while retaining the union of the UK.

In considering the various options outlined in this chapter, it is important to be clear what the purpose of more devolution is. All of the schemes discussed would result in a greater part of Scottish public expenditure being financed by taxes paid in Scotland and would therefore improve accountability. But what is it that the advocates of more devolution actually want? Probably more control over the policies that are applied to Scotland; and, while the increased tax-raising powers under these schemes make possible a different spread of taxation according to income, they do not do as much to make possible the substantial differences in policy that some people may wish. Even with a devolved constitution, however, there is much that a Scottish Government could do, but has not so far done, to promote the growth of the economy. The last section of this chapter considers this before, in the next chapter, going on to discuss the additional scope that might be available to an independent Scotland.

Economic Policy with Devolution

The Scottish Government already has substantial responsibilities for areas of policy that can affect the growth of the economy. Assistance for economic development, education and skill training, and infrastructure investment are devolved responsibilities. All of these are of the greatest importance for the performance of the economy.

Vocational skill training seems to have been treated as the poor relation of university education and has tended to suffer in consequence, not only in Scotland but also in the UK as a whole. Increasing the number of university graduates is important for the economy and is to be welcomed, but the economy also depends on a good supply of school leavers who acquire high quality vocational skills. The Scottish Government recently decided to reduce funding for further education colleges while, at the same time, adhering to the policy of free university education for Scottish students at Scottish universities, despite the decisions of the other countries in the UK to charge fees. This decision has raised doubts over whether its priorities on higher and further education or skill training have been properly assessed.

When compared with some other parts of the UK, an important feature of the Scottish economy has been the relatively poor growth from new business start-ups and from small business. Scottish Enterprise and the SDA before it have given a lot of attention to fostering business start-ups and encouraging the growth of small firms. But it is not easy – a lot of small businesses fail and whether others succeed may depend heavily on the support they get. This was a large part of the rationale for setting up the SDA in 1975. It was believed at that time that there was a shortage of equity finance for small businesses. This, it was argued, made them too heavily dependent on bank finance in the form of loans and so gave them insufficient flexibility to survive fluctuations in the market.

There have been many improvements to the availability of equity finance since the SDA was set up. But, following the financial crisis of the last few years, funding from the banks has become much harder to obtain, as their priority has been to rebuild their balance sheets and increase their capital. This makes it all the more important that the Scottish Government, probably through Scottish Enterprise and Highlands and Islands Enterprise, gives close attention to the needs of small businesses, both in the provision of advice and in meeting their financial needs.

Many entrepreneurs start businesses nowadays with an eye to an eventual exit, often taking the form of takeover by a larger group. There is nothing wrong with that – indeed, without it, there would be less business formation. What can be more problematic is the takeover of much larger, longer-established UK companies. Obviously there are times when a company is struggling and takeover by a competitor or a large firm is the only way to save the business. Or the company may be stagnating under current management and the shareholders take the view that a change in control is the way to avoid eventual decline. There are also cases where a takeover or merger, whether originated by a Scottish firm or a firm outside Scotland, is desirable and in Scotland's interest. It can open up new opportunities or add valuable strength to an existing operation.

But there are many examples where there has been little or no economic advantage in a change of ownership or control. In Scotland, the takeover of Scottish and Newcastle Breweries by Heineken and Carlsberg in 2008 is an example of one that only took place because shareholders saw the prospect of a short-term gain in a higher share price. Sometimes, fear that they will be taken over prompts the management of a successful firm to try to take over others to prevent it being taken over itself. The clearest examples of this are the two Scottish banks. As Ray Perman's recent book on the Bank of Scotland makes clear, the disastrous merger of the Bank of Scotland with the Halifax largely came about because the Bank of Scotland management felt they were at risk if the bank remained independent.[18] In the case of the Royal Bank also, though there were certainly other factors, fear of takeover was probably in the minds of the board in trying to make the bank a bigger and yet bigger business.

Norman Tebbit, when UK Secretary of State for Trade and Industry in the 1980s, removed from the rules for appraising takeovers the clause that required the authorities to take into account regional implications. This was unfortunate. It was done after the successful defence of the Royal Bank's independence (which was unpopular in some quarters in London) against the proposal for merger with Standard Chartered Bank in 1981 and the counter bid of Hongkong and Shanghai Banking Corporation. The regional implications need to be restored to the appraisal of such takeovers, not only for Scotland but for other parts of the UK as well. If the Scottish economy is to prosper, companies headquartered in Scotland should be protected from aggressive takeovers carried out only for shareholders' short-term gain or for the aggrandisement of management. The conclusion must surely be that takeovers are too easy and that an opportunity should be given for the long-term costs and benefits to the economy to be properly considered, perhaps going so far as to refuse to allow a takeover or merger to proceed where the parties cannot show these benefits. But it is not easy to see how such a change in policy could be effective, unless it was done for the UK as a whole. It, therefore, requires determined lobbying by the Scottish Government.

In respect of all the issues set out above – vocational training, support and finance for new and small business, and takeovers – the Scottish Government could learn much from Germany. The German economy has the largest and strongest manufacturing sector in Europe; the training of apprentices is well organised and few school leavers are without either further education or training. The *Mittelstand*, the small- and medium-sized business sector in Germany, has been an outstandingly important feature of the economy and it depends in large degree for its success on its close links with financial institutions. A longer-term view on the part of both business and finance has resulted in the takeover frenzy that has been such a feature of Britain being much less evident in the German economy.

Devolution could, therefore, be increased and developed to provide greater accountability for the Scottish Parliament and much greater policy responsibility for the Scottish Government in raising the revenue to finance its expenditure. And there are also policies that the Scottish Government could adopt, even with its existing powers but increasingly so with more financial powers, to promote the growth of the economy.

Currency and Taxes: The Scope for an Independent Economic Policy

The last chapter discussed the scope for greater economic powers for the Scottish Parliament under various schemes for devolution. As I argued in that chapter, there is much that a devolved administration can or could do, and Scotland's Parliament could be responsible for raising more of the tax revenue to finance its expenditure. But the scope for independence in managing the economy would be limited. This is especially so as fiscal, monetary and exchange rate policies would all be reserved to the UK Government. The essence of macroeconomic policy is the ability to budget for a surplus or a deficit, so as to control inflation and stimulate economic growth. Policy to deal with these matters would inevitably remain with the UK Government.

With independence these constraints theoretically disappear, and Scottish Ministers have claimed that only independence would give them the levers they need to manage the economy in the interests of the Scottish people. So far they have not been very specific about these levers or how they would use them. This chapter, therefore, tries to examine how valid this assertion is. But, in practical terms, no government can pursue policies regardless of what its neighbours and trading partners are doing. All economies nowadays are interdependent, as can readily be seen from the effect on the UK of policies in the United States and the

European Union. This would be especially so for Scotland, given its relatively small size, the fact that the rest of the UK would be its dominant trading partner, that it has been integrated as part of the UK for so long and that freedom of movement of both capital and labour throughout the single market of the present UK would continue.

No one is suggesting that Scotland could not manage its economy successfully if it became independent; certainly, I do not argue that. Scotland, as I have shown in Chapter 1, is quite a wealthy country and has many strengths in its economy. Furthermore there are reasons for thinking that independent states can sometimes perform better economically than regions of larger countries. This is most obviously so where the economic structure and relative wealth of the area, and that of the economy with which it might be joined, are very different. This has been a concern with the expansion of the EU, where the economies of, say, Greece and Bulgaria are very different from that of Germany or France. It is because of this that the EU has set up the structural funds and particularly the cohesion fund to help countries and regions with their development.

A useful starting point is perhaps to consider how the Republic of Ireland might have done, had it remained part of the UK. Certainly its recent financial crisis as an independent country within the eurozone would have been less severe as part of the UK. The most significant difference would have been that Ireland would have had the backing of a larger state to support it. It is also argued, with some justification, that its housing boom would not have got so completely out of hand if it had not joined the euro, although it was bad enough in the UK itself.

As an independent country since 1922, Ireland had a shaky start and a long period of economic stagnation until at least the early 1960s. The turning point only came when policies were adopted that resulted in much faster growth, especially in the late 1970s, 1980s and into the 1990s. From having a GDP per head that had been only about half the UK average in the 1950s, it was matching, if not exceeding, the UK GDP per head by the 1990s. It does not seem likely that Ireland could have achieved that, had it remained a region of the UK, even if it had benefitted from UK regional policy and generous financial support.

The Irish success was mainly due to an ability to match policies to the specific needs of the Irish economy, which were different to the UK, and in particular its success in attracting inward investment. For this its Industrial Development Agency and very generous incentives, including but not exclusively an exceptionally low rate of Corporation Tax, are responsible. Since 1973, it has also received considerable help as a member state of the EU.

Perhaps the most important policy lever that independent states have, however, though not one used by Ireland, is the ability for the exchange rate of an independent currency to adjust so that the economy remains competitive. Independent states have to balance their payments with the rest of the world and exchange rate adjustment is the principal mechanism by which this is done. Once a state establishes itself with a competitive exchange rate, investment is encouraged, the economy can grow and unemployment can be eliminated. For this reason it is unusual for advanced countries, even small ones, to have persistently high unemployment or emigration. But a fall in the exchange rate involves a cut in living standards. This may be only temporary, if the economy responds with higher economic growth, increased investment and higher employment; but reality does not always accord with theory. Devaluations are not always effective and they may lead to higher inflation, if they are followed by wage pressure to restore previous living standards.

There are exceptions, therefore, to the success of independent states and much depends on the way the economy is managed. The existence of one very strong sector, such as one based on a valuable natural resource, can drive up the exchange rate, adversely affecting the rest of the economy – the so-called 'resource curse' referred to in Chapter 1. This calls for intelligent policies to manage it. Norway is an example of a country that has done this well following the discovery of North Sea oil and gas, but the other small Scandinavian countries without this resource also have successful economies and are often referred to by advocates of Scottish independence.

A region of a larger state lacks this mechanism of adjustment if its industries decline or become less competitive, or where economic performance lags behind the rest of the state. Where there is no separate currency and an exchange rate that can adjust, pressure to reduce wages and living standards, such as is happening now in some eurozone countries, can achieve the same result. But it is a slow and very painful process, even in economies where wages and other costs are flexible. It may be strongly resisted by trades unions and by the public generally.

Britain, especially in the 1960s and 1970s, developed regional policies to tackle these problems in parts of the country where there was a need for readjustment resulting from the decline of older industries and in rising unemployment; these policies provided grants to assist industrial investment and in Scotland led to the setting up of the Scottish Development Agency (now Scottish Enterprise). The result was considerable success, especially in attracting international investment, where Scotland was second only to the Republic of Ireland. Regional policy has been greatly weakened, however, since the 1980s; it has been out of favour with those who strongly oppose anything that interferes with the operation of the free market. But meanwhile the problem of regional imbalance persists and has even increased, especially as it affects the north of England and Wales. At the other extreme, the London economy and that of the southeast of England have become ever more prosperous, based to a large extent on the phenomenal growth of the financial sector.

A country that has been part of a larger state but becomes independent is not in the same position as one that has been independent all along because it is highly integrated with the larger entity. Independence will, therefore, involve costs arising from disruption. The more integrated it is, the greater these costs may be, and this is likely to give rise to adverse consequences that may last for a considerable time. In arguing for independence, the SNP Government recognises this, which is why its policies are aimed at causing the minimum disruption. Nevertheless the economic case for independence rests on the ability to use levers or adopt policies that would only be available to an independent state.

The policies mentioned in the white paper are a lower rate of Corporation Tax than elsewhere in the UK and targeted depreciation allowances; strengthening the role of the Scottish Investment Bank; reduced air passenger duty; support for small and medium enterprises; maximising investment, with particular attention to research and development; action on employment regulation and the minimum wage; a youth guarantee to provide opportunity of education, training or employment as a constitutional right; and an effective immigration policy based on a points system to meet Scotland's needs. Since the white paper was published, the SNP Government has also committed itself to much expanded childcare to free young mothers to join the labour force. A number of these policies could be adopted under devolution, as the last chapter has shown. The main areas of policy that affect the country's economic growth, however, are fiscal policy, monetary policy and decisions on currency.

This chapter, therefore, considers these in turn. It concludes by considering whether the painful austerity of recent years could have been avoided and whether independence could have given a Scottish government power to follow a different course.

Fiscal Policy

An independent Scotland would raise all of its own tax revenue, including personal taxation, VAT, excise duties and Corporation Tax; it would have to decide what rates should be set for each tax. It would also be responsible for all of its public expenditure, including defence, foreign embassies and interest on the national debt, items that are at present dealt with centrally by the UK.

But there would still be constraints. Differences in VAT or in excise duties, although allowed for individual states under EU rules, could, if substantial, encourage trading across the border, as happens now with alcohol between Britain and Continental countries. Differences in personal taxation, especially for those with higher incomes who move easily, would carry a risk that some people, valuable to the economy for their skill or entrepreneurship, would vote with their feet, moving either to or from Scotland; and the integration of the UK labour market, including the absence of any language barrier, such as applies in other EU states, would make it very easy for people to move to wherever gave them most opportunity. I suspect, however, that differences in personal tax would have to be significant, certainly larger than present differences in Council Tax, for this to become an issue.

Differences in rates of Corporation Tax exist between EU

countries. But, if the Scottish Government tried, as is its stated aim,[1] to reduce the rate of tax to a very low level, or as stated in the white paper[2] to 3 per cent below the UK rate, which is itself much lower than the rate of Corporation Tax in Germany or many other EU countries, it could be seen as an attempt not just to help companies in Scotland, but to attract economic activity that might otherwise go elsewhere in the UK or to other member states of the EU. That would raise problems both with the European Union and the remainder of the UK. As it is, several EU countries have taken issue with Ireland's low 12.5 per cent rate of Corporation Tax, notably at the time of the Irish financial bailout, arguing that it was unacceptably distorting. While Ireland has, so far, managed to resist this pressure, it is unlikely that a newly independent Scotland, seeking to establish itself within the EU, would be able to do so.

Moreover, as a response to the difficulties in the eurozone, proposals are being developed that would include a banking union and much greater integration of fiscal policy for countries in the zone. This will apparently give members of the zone some oversight of each other's budgets, with the intention of ensuring that they all pursue policies of financial rectitude. It is not clear at present how far this will go or whether it will be acceptable to member states; but it is likely to increase pressure for greater harmonisation of taxes, including Corporation Tax, even for countries that are not in the eurozone but are part of the EU.

The Importance of North Sea Oil Revenues

The inclusion of the North Sea on a geographical basis makes a substantial difference to the size of the Scottish economy. As we have seen in Chapter 1, it would immediately add about 21 per cent to Scotland's GDP.[3] It would also provide a large flow of taxation revenue and such revenue would be a much larger component of a Scottish Government's budget than it has been of the budget of the UK. Its contribution to the balance of payments would also be very important; and, if there were a separate Scottish currency, its value would be heavily influenced by the price and volume of oil produced. The problem (as will be seen from the graphs in Chapter 7) is that the value of the oil and gas produced has fluctuated over the years, not just because output has varied but even more because prices have been volatile.

The implications of North Sea oil revenues for the balance of payments and the exchange rate (if Scotland had its own currency) are considerable and could be the opposite of those for the government's budget. The higher the revenues, the more the Scottish Government's budget would gain. But the balance of payments on foreign transactions is a different matter. A high oil price and, consequently, high revenues carry the danger that, by generating a large balance of payments surplus, they could push the exchange rate up, thereby threatening damage to the non-oil economy. This is not a minor concern, as has already been explained. The Dutch economy suffered in the 1970s when discoveries of natural gas threatened to damage non-gas-related activities; this became known as 'the Dutch disease'. In the same way, the massive growth in UK oil revenues in the early 1980s was one of the factors that brought about a very sharp rise in the sterling exchange rate, which, in turn, was a major factor in the recession of those years and caused the loss of a lot of manufacturing industry.* The Scottish Government would therefore have to stand ready to counteract this effect by investing abroad, as Norway has done with its oil

---

* This effect was, of course, compounded by the very tight monetary policy adopted by the UK Government in the early 1980s.

fund, or by some other means, if the rest of the economy was being affected. The danger that fluctuating oil revenue may cause these problems is probably one reason why the SNP Government does not want to sever the link with sterling; however, there could still be major implications for the budget, with high revenues resulting in a budget surplus and low revenues in a deficit. It is also one reason why the Government's Fiscal Commission advocates setting up an oil fund, which would be used to provide greater stability, a subject that is discussed further in Chapter 7.

The Scottish electorate will therefore have to decide whether it will take the risk that there may be times when, perhaps because of a drop in oil revenues or some other reason, taxation revenue falls and public expenditure has to be cut to match it. Those arguing for independence or some form of complete fiscal autonomy for Scotland, such as Devo-Max, need to face up to this issue.

Monetary Policy and the Choice of Currency

The Scottish Government said in the white paper that it would be its intention to keep sterling as the national currency after independence and that the monetary union with the rest of the UK would therefore continue. That was also the recommendation of the Scottish Government's Fiscal Commission.[4] But as this book went to press, George Osborne, the Chancellor of the Exchequer in a speech in Edinburgh ruled this out as impractical. In this he was supported by Ed Balls, the Labour Shadow Chancellor, and Danny Alexander, the Liberal Democrat Chief Secretary at the Treasury. On the same day, however, in *The Scotsman*, the Fiscal Commission's view has been reiterated by Sir James Mirrlees, emeritus professor of economics at Cambridge and Nobel prize-winner in economics. He refers to the burden of transaction costs that businesses on both sides of the border would suffer in the absence of such a union, but emphasises the need for financial stability and a consistent regulatory structure. While the Chancellor's intervention does not rule out some form of monetary union, it does make a formal, fully integrated union with the Bank of England continuing as central bank and lender of last resort for both countries extremely unlikely. A host of questions therefore follow.

Mark Carney, the Governor of the Bank of England, in a speech in Edinburgh earlier, while not ruling monetary union out, pointed out that to work it would mean a significant surrender of sovereignty. Citing the examples of monetary union in Canada and the United States, he pointed out that a fully integrated monetary union worked best where a large part of fiscal policy was also integrated so that if part of the union suffered a severe shock to its economy, such as the collapse of an industry, other parts of the union would automatically provide support. Brian Quinn, a former Deputy Governor of the Bank of England, has argued in a paper for the David Hume Institute that there are difficulties in having a central bank responsible to two separate parliaments. Indeed his view was that it would be unworkable.[5]

Scottish Ministers have suggested that if the rest of the UK refuses monetary union for Scotland, the Scottish Government could refuse to take a share of the UK national debt. No doubt this is intended as some kind of bargaining counter. But it is rash and irresponsible. If Scotland refused to take its share of the debt, this would be regarded by many people, and most importantly by the markets, as equivalent to a default. That would be held against Scotland in any negotiations to enter or remain in the EU. It would also mean a loss of trust by the markets in any Scottish bonds that the Government issued. This would raise interest rates on Scottish debt, causing severe difficulty for any borrowing. Moreover, the rest of the UK, with which the Scottish Government would inevitably have to negotiate the terms of its independence, would seek to retaliate by raising difficulties over other matters. This does not seem a sensible course to follow.

What then are the possibilities? It has been suggested that the Scottish Government might continue to use sterling on an informal basis, as Panama and Hong Kong use the US dollar. But to use sterling without a lender of last resort to help Scottish banks if they get into difficulty and without any influence at all on monetary policies followed by the Bank of England, would be dangerous and much less satisfactory than at present as part of the UK union.

But no formal currency union does not mean no monetary union. Even with an informal monetary union there would probably have to be a Scottish currency and either a currency board to manage it or a Scottish central bank. Before they joined the euro Belgium and Luxembourg had been in currency union for many years without any apparent difficulty. Like the rest of the UK and Scotland, there was a large disparity in the population of the two countries. Both countries issued their own currency notes. This meant that they had separate currencies but that their exchange value was pegged. This type of arrangement works best where the smaller country, which has to keep it currency in step with the larger, has only a small national debt. That certainly is the case in both Luxembourg and Hong Kong. Provided that the currency notes are able to be exchanged at par, those issued in either country can be freely used in the other. But this is not an essential condition. One can imagine a monetary union of this type working even where the notes were of different values and not so easily exchangeable, although that would impose additional costs on those trading between the two countries.

Here the experience of Ireland is interesting, although the present circumstances of Scotland and those of the then Irish Free State in 1922 are very different. After independence, Ireland retained sterling as its currency and the Irish banks, like Scottish banks now, continued to issue notes of their own, which were accepted as sterling both by businesses and members of the public, but were fully backed by deposits at the Bank of England. The first Irish Banking Commission set up in 1926 proposed introducing Ireland's own currency but emphasised the importance of retaining the 1:1 parity with sterling. These notes were, therefore, exchangeable at par with Bank of England notes and were managed by an Irish Currency Commission. Ireland did not actually get a central bank until 1943, following the Central Bank Act of 1942. The remarkable consequence of all this was that, in the absence of any formal agreement with the Bank of England, Ireland was without a lender of last resort for some 21 years. This is particularly surprising when one considers that those years included the 1930s depression, a trade war with the UK and the first four years of a world war.

Mercifully, this need did not arise, as no Irish banks got into trouble during this time and successive governments operated extremely conservative fiscal policies. With much greater speculative activity now an important and unavoidable feature of financial markets, it is hard to see an independent Scotland getting away with having no lender of last resort. Nor, one imagines, would an independent Scotland, trying to stimulate its economy and wanting to use fiscal levers for this purpose, be content with an extremely conservative fiscal policy of the kind followed by Ireland after independence. But, with a deficit of 5.0 per cent of GDP in 2011–12 (even including a geographical share of North Sea revenues), there would anyway hardly be scope for an expansionary fiscal policy.

Was Ireland right to follow this policy of retaining the link with sterling through thick and thin? Successive experts, including the First Banking Commission and the majority report of the Second, argued strongly for this. But the minority report of the Second Commission disagreed, saying that they could not:

> acquiesce in the extraordinary view that this country, alone among responsible entities in the world, should not ever have the power to make decisions, and that no apparatus or mechanism for controlling the volume and direction of credit should ever be brought into existence.[6]

Nowadays there are some in Ireland who strongly criticise the policies pursued in the early decades after its independence. Conor McCabe, for example, argues forcefully that, given the poor and underdeveloped state of the Irish economy at that time, retaining an overvalued currency, which is what the parity link with sterling implied, was profoundly damaging to the economy and was one of the factors that led to Ireland's relative stagnation during that time.[7]

What is clear is that even if the UK were to relent and allowed an independent Scotland to continue to use sterling, there would have to be Scottish Government bonds to cover its borrowing, and this would certainly be required in any looser form of monetary union. Such bonds would probably require a higher interest rate than bonds of the rest of the UK, until the market was satisfied, as a result of experience, that they were safe and backed by a lender of last resort.

So there is much that would need to be decided and many issues that have not as yet been discussed. If Scotland does become independent, my own view is that it should continue in some form of monetary union with the rest of the UK, if it can. It is possible that some form of transitional arrangement could be negotiated with the rest of the UK, until Scotland had its own central bank and was able to issue currency notes. But the constraints would be considerable during this time, even if the UK Government and the Bank of England were receptive to what Scotland wanted.

It is interesting to note that, when the Czech and the Slovak republics split in 1993, before they joined the EU, they intended to maintain monetary union and a common currency at least initially, though with the prospect that they might adopt their own separate currencies eventually. In the event, the monetary union collapsed in less than six weeks, as a large volume of funds flowed from Slovakia into banks in the Czech Republic. Controls on capital movements had to be imposed and the existing Czechoslovak currency was over-stamped by each country to distinguish it, until two new currencies could be introduced. The lesson is that, if the markets think a monetary union will not last, it becomes very difficult and costly to maintain and it will, in the end, fail. So, if there were a period of uncertainty about currency arrangements after a YES vote in the referendum, it could lead to bank deposits being moved out of Scotland for greater security and a movement of funds into secure sterling bonds. That could force a break-up of the monetary union, despite what the Scottish Government wanted or planned.

Whatever the outcome, it would seem that a Scottish central bank would have to be set up, and this would be a requirement anyhow for a member state of the EU. A separate central bank would not mean the end of sterling monetary union – indeed, the eurozone countries all have their own central banks. But, if Scotland's central bank was to be given power to act as lender of last resort – and my view is that it should have such power – it would have to have a separate currency as well. This could be pegged to sterling or indeed the euro, depending on circumstances, just as monetary union continued with Ireland up to 1978.

There would be considerable advantages in maintaining some form of monetary union, as the Scottish Government's Fiscal Commission argues, if that can be done on acceptable terms, given the closely integrated nature of the Scottish economy with the rest of the present UK and the fact that so many financial institutions based in Scotland do most of their business south of the border.[8] As I argue in Chapter 9, there would also be implications for mortgages and pensions, if Scotland had a separate currency. But, as Professor John Kay (formerly a member of the First Minister's Council of Economic Advisers) recently said in a lecture at Glasgow University, the Scottish Government's freedom of action to tailor policy to Scottish needs – the economic levers about which politicians so frequently speak – would be constrained.[9] In order to gain more flexibility this could eventually induce a Scottish government to break any currency link and have a totally independent Scottish currency.

The importance of having a separate note issue, even if pegged to sterling, is that it would make it possible to avoid the type of disaster – stemming from loss of competitiveness – that has affected the countries of southern Europe within the eurozone. Some smaller countries in Europe that still have their own currencies – Denmark being one obvious example – have found that it makes sense to shadow the currency of a larger area, usually the euro. But this still gives them freedom, *in extremis*, to allow their currencies to be revalued either up or down, should the need arise. They are not locked into a monetary union from which they cannot escape. This may mean that interest rates are slightly higher than for the currency that is being shadowed, because of exchange rate risk, but the kind of problems that are now so distressingly evident in

Spain, Portugal, Italy and Greece could be avoided, or at least substantially mitigated.

So there would be important decisions to be taken on the currency and on how a Scottish Government would manage its budget. We need a clearer statement from the Government about the additional levers it seeks and how it would use them. It is unfortunate, in my opinion, that the Government's white paper gives no indication of a fall-back policy – or plan B – if the policy to which it has committed itself, of full monetary union and the Bank of England acting for both countries, proves unacceptable. Trying to continue with sterling with no agreement, as some have suggested, is not a practical proposition: it would deprive Scotland of any influence on monetary policy and there would be no lender of last resort. Joining the eurozone instead is discussed in the next chapter, but that does not seem to me a desirable course either. So the only plan B, and the outcome which I expect eventually, if not at the start, would be for Scotland to have its own central bank and its own currency. This should probably be pegged to sterling, but the flexibility would be there to alter the exchange rate, if that proved really necessary, in the interests of the economy. This would also give Scotland greater, though still limited, scope in fiscal policy, which the Scottish Government clearly want.

Could the Austerity of the Last Few Years Have Been Avoided?

What, I suspect, supporters of independence or much greater devolution would really like is a government that has the power to do things differently from the rest of the UK in ways that would improve the quality of their lives. The austerity policies of the present UK Government are a case in point. These policies have been controversial and have resulted in both hardship and unemployment.

There can be no dispute about the need for a country to be able to live within its means over the longer term. Neither the UK nor Scotland is doing that at present, as can be seen from their unsustainable budget deficits (see Chapter 1) and the consequent rise in the UK national debt. But political independence has not saved other countries from similar trouble.

I am among those who think that Chancellor George Osborne's policies have been needlessly harsh. He has failed to meet his targets either for eliminating the budget deficit before the next election or to have the national debt falling by then. Austerity is now to be extended well beyond the term of the present Westminster Parliament. All of this stems from the banking crisis of 2007–08 (I discuss the difficulties that Scotland might have had in handling that in Chapter 5). The problem now is how to get the country back to a position where it is living within its means.

To many people and, it seems, to some politicians, a government deficit is seen as analogous to an individual spending more than he or she earns. The only solution, then, is to reduce spending so that it no longer exceeds income. But, for a country, the analogy is misleading. Cutting public spending and raising taxes affect the level of activity in the economy. This causes unemployment and expenditure on benefits to rise and taxation revenue to fall. The policy will, therefore, only succeed if these secondary effects are smaller than the initial gain to the budget's balance from the cut in expenditure or higher taxes.

This is what economists call the fiscal multiplier. If the multiplier is low, the secondary effects will be modest and the attempt to get the budget back into balance by cutting expenditure or raising taxes will have a good chance of success. But if the multiplier is high, the secondary effects can nullify much of what policy is trying to achieve and a downward spiral may develop. This is what seems to be happening in certain eurozone countries and has happened, to some extent, in the UK.

It seems that there was a serious misjudgement over the size of the fiscal multiplier at the start. Initially, it was thought to be low (about 0.5, meaning that, for a 1 per cent cut in public expenditure or increased tax, there would be a half per cent reduction in GDP growth).[10] But that was based on research done in normal times and more recent research by the International Monetary Fund has concluded that the fiscal multiplier is now much higher (in the range 0.9–1.7).[11] This is because, in normal times, a tightening of fiscal policy can be offset by a relaxation in monetary policy. Also, the earlier calculation assumed that the policy was applied by one country in isolation. In present conditions, with Bank of England interest rates at their lowest ever level, monetary policy cannot be relaxed further and almost all of Europe and the United States are trying to cut their budget deficits simultaneously. As each country does this, imports from other countries are reduced and the consequence of so many countries attempting this together increases the depressive effect. Action taken to reduce the budget deficit has, therefore, had a much greater impact on growth than anticipated and this, in turn, makes it much more difficult to get the budget into balance.

In an important paper, Dawn Holland and Jonathan Portes of the National Institute for Economic and Social Research conclude that the poor growth performance of most EU countries, including the UK, during this recession can be attributed to the attempts at fiscal consolidation. This is because of the spill-over effects from one country to another of the action taken and the inability of monetary policy to compensate.[12] These negative effects have been larger than governments expected. They might have been less if policy had been aimed at measures with a lower multiplier. These might include an increase in Income Tax, rather than VAT, because it would have more impact on higher income groups, who do not spend so much of their income, and cuts in current public spending being at least partially offset by increased infrastructure investment that can yield a return. The most important lesson, perhaps, is that countries are now so interdependent and the spill-over effects from one country to another so great that the most effective policy would be a programme of actions carefully co-ordinated between countries. It might have resulted in higher borrowing in the short term but the ratio of national debt to GDP would have stopped rising sooner, as the economy's growth began to pick up.

What are the implications of all this for an independent Scotland? The fiscal multiplier is not the same for all countries. Small open economies, such as Scotland's, will have a lower multiplier than large, more self-sufficient ones because so much of the depressive effect of cuts in public spending or increases in taxes will hit imports. While the adverse effect on growth of trying to balance its budget would be relatively small for a Scottish Government acting on its own, the spill-over effects from and to other countries would be very large. This conclusion is not very surprising. It means that what a Scottish Government could do to stave off the adverse effects on its economy of an attempt by the UK and other countries to get their budgets into balance would be very limited. Inevitably, the Scottish economy would be very dependent on policies adopted by its trading partners, whatever the constitutional arrangement.

Conclusion

What the government of an independent Scotland could do in economic policy would certainly be less restricted than what would be possible under any of the proposed schemes of devolution. But there would still be constraints, depending on the outcome of negotiations with the rest of the UK. This applies particularly to the SNP Government's expressed intention to retain sterling as the currency for an independent Scotland. Obviously this would preclude any independent monetary or exchange rate policy. The government's white paper assumes that the Bank of England would not only remain the central bank for both countries but also that it would continue to act as lender of last resort for Scotland. This may not be possible. This reasoning leads to the conclusion that there ought to be, if not immediately, then in due course, a Scottish central bank; this is likely, anyway, to be a condition of EU membership. If the Scottish central bank was to have lender of last resort powers, that would require a Scottish currency, which could be linked to sterling.

But monetary union would also impose tight restrictions on fiscal policy. Two issues arise here. Scotland and the rest of the UK would have to be satisfied on the sustainability of each other's deficit and debt management. This means that the size of any budget deficit would have to be acceptable, but experience has shown that is far from enough. A major recession can force an increase in deficits regardless of government intentions, both because of an unanticipated collapse in tax revenue, and because of an unavoidable increase in benefit expenditure as unemployment rises. This also implies a need for agreement on the scale of personal and mortgage debt, which have been major factors in the UK and US recessions, and in several other EU countries.

The other issue on which agreement would most probably be required if monetary union was to be acceptable to both Scotland and the rest of the UK would be the avoidance of discriminatory taxation that caused economic distortion in favour of either partner. Here the biggest problem, potentially, at least, would arise from significant differences in Corporation Tax, which could make it impossible to negotiate monetary union on the basis set out in the white paper.

The SNP Government has not so far specified how it would use its greater powers or the levers it would acquire with independence to achieve faster economic growth for Scotland. This is so central to the economic case for independence that more explanation is urgently required for this case to be convincing.

There is so much in both monetary and fiscal policy that would depend on the success or otherwise of negotiations with the government of the remainder of the UK that, as several commentators have said, an alternative plan – a plan B – is badly needed, in case agreement on full monetary union proves impossible or only possible on terms that are too restrictive to be accepted. Such a plan B should involve Scotland having its own central bank and its own currency, if it was to act as lender of last resort. A Scottish currency could, however, be pegged to sterling for as long as that seemed the best policy, and that would not require the agreement of the remainder of the UK.

Scotland and Europe

Scotland's position in Europe, if it becomes independent, is of major importance to the economy because of the large amount of international investment that has come here and which, it is hoped, will continue to come. Much of the economy depends on it and it provides a lot of employment. It is not surprising, therefore, that the issue has generated a lot of debate. The SNP Government was clearly at fault in its original claim that Scotland would automatically remain a member of the EU. The First Minister gave the impression that his Government had received legal advice on the issue, but it then transpired it had no such advice. This was a shambles. The UK Government, on the other hand, said that Scotland, as a newly independent state, would be outside the EU and would have to apply for membership in the same way as any other candidate state. This was confirmed by José Manuel Barroso, the President of the European Commission, in a letter to the House of Lords Economic Affairs Committee. The Spanish Prime Minister, Mariano Rajoy, has also entered the debate in support of Mr Barroso's and the UK Government's view, no doubt with an eye on the implications for Catalonia, where there is also a movement for secession.

The UK Government, in support of its view, has published the detailed opinion it obtained from two experts in international law, Professors James Crawford of Cambridge and Alan Boyle of Edinburgh University.[1] They argue that Scotland would be treated much as any other state wanting membership, which would require a treaty of accession. There is no precedent in international law. No part of an existing member state has become independent before and then applied for membership in its own right. There is, therefore, no recognised procedure that meets the case.

On the other hand, Sir David Edward, the distinguished Scottish former judge at the European Court of Justice, who in that capacity was regularly involved in the interpretation of the EU Treaties, has taken a different view. He points out that, as there is provision under article 50 of the Treaty of Lisbon for a member state to withdraw from the EU and likewise provision for a process of negotiation and agreement in such circumstances, it would be contrary to the spirit of the Treaties to suddenly treat Scotland as outside the EU, if by popular referendum it chose to become a separate state.* He also points out that 'Article 2 of the Treaty on European Union affirms the belief that the Union is founded on certain core values, including respect for human dignity, freedom and democracy. If the majority were to vote for independence, it is difficult to see why those core values should not be respected.' He also says, 'It is not obvious . . . why the EU should hold open its doors to small nations of Middle and Eastern Europe, whose very existence as independent states is due to the break-up of greater entities, while slamming them shut against the aspirations of those who regard themselves as "stateless nations" in Western Europe.' In expressing these views, he makes it clear that his own position is that of a 'moderate unionist'.

What seems to me the key point here is that, if leaving the EU involves negotiation, then Scotland's circumstance must also be the subject of negotiation during the period between

* Sir David Edward has dealt with the issues comprehensively in his paper *EU Law and the Separation of Member States*, Fordham University International Law Journal, Vol. 36.5, p. 2 ff.

the referendum vote and the moment when separation takes effect. Sir David concludes that the result of negotiation could be treaty amendment rather than a new accession treaty, which would involve delay and could require Scotland to take its place in a queue behind other applicant states. But he points out that the key is the good faith of other member states (including the United Kingdom) until the moment of separation.

All these views are, of course, those of experts and are based on experience. I claim no legal expertise, but I find Sir David's view persuasive. To argue otherwise would mean that, at the time of separation from the rest of the UK, all existing arrangements with the EU, including, presumably, grants from the Structural Funds, the Common Agricultural Policy (CAP) payments, provision for Erasmus students and access in Scottish territorial waters for fishermen of other member states, would suddenly end. That would not happen even to a country that wished to leave the EU. It seems very clear that there would be negotiations and it is hard to see why Scotland could not have its situation dealt with by a treaty amendment, as Sir David argues. Whichever course is followed, the main difference between a treaty amendment and a new treaty of accession is in the time it might take and the extent of the upheaval. If Sir David is right, it might be accomplished quite quickly, within the two or more years between the referendum result and actual separation from the rest of the UK. All are agreed, however, that the agreement of all existing 28 member states would be required, any one of whom could exercise a veto.

The issue is of major importance, especially for business. Many of the inward investment companies that decided to come to Scotland did so because they saw it as a good base from which to serve the large EU market. Scotland had what they needed – good sites for development, a supply of excellent labour, including graduates, and a dependable political and legal environment. Those that came from the United States and Japan also probably found it helpful that the language they needed was English, since that has become the international language for business. If, therefore, access from Scotland to the European single market was now to appear to be at risk, not only would it be hard to attract more investment from abroad, but companies already here might begin to think of moving elsewhere. Ireland is Scotland's main competitor for such investment and its position as a member of the EU is quite secure.

There are some who have argued that, if Scotland becomes independent, it would mean repealing the 1707 Act of Union, and that Scotland and the rest of the UK would then be in exactly the same position as new states. They then assert that, if Scotland has to apply for EU membership as a new state, so would the remainder of the UK. This raises the question of whether one of or both Scotland and the remainder of the UK would be treated as successor states, an issue which Sir David also deals with in the paper already referred to. In the case of the break-up of Czechoslovakia, both the Czech Republic and Slovakia were treated as successor states for the treaties that the previous combined state had signed, though they were not in the EU at the time. However, not only was the split mutually agreed but the two countries were much more equal in size than Scotland and the remainder of the UK.

In Scotland's case neither of these circumstances would apply. Scotland would be by far the smaller state and the issue would only arise because of its decision in a referendum to secede from the UK, not any decision taken by the electorate in the rest of the UK. The view of the experts who have dealt with the issue is, therefore, that the rest of the UK would be the successor state and would inherit all the treaties signed by it before Scotland seceded. It would, however, have to face some, *probably* slight, adjustment to its terms of EU membership on such matters as the number of MEPs and its budget rebate, as it would no longer be a country of 63 million people. Scotland would be the new state and would have to negotiate with the EU afresh to decide its conditions of membership. This would include its voting rights, its number of MEPs and whether or not it sought the same derogations as the UK. Lord Kerr of Kinlochard, former head of the Foreign Office, Ambassador and UK Representative to the European Union, has warned that Scotland might find it difficult to obtain the same terms and opt-outs as have been available to it as part of the UK.[2]

Scotland has been in the EU for 40 years as part of the UK and there is, therefore, no question that it satisfies the criteria for membership; but there are the derogations the UK already has from the EU treaties, enabling it to exclude itself from joining the euro or the border-free Schengen Area. The question arises over whether these could be retained by Scotland. Like the rest of the UK, Scotland has also shared in the budgetary rebate negotiated by Mrs Thatcher, as UK Prime Minister, at Fontainebleau in 1984.

Schengen

Securing an opt-out from the Schengen Area seems likely to be the least difficult of these problems. The Schengen Agreement was originally independent of the EU but was absorbed into EU law by the Amsterdam Treaty of 1997. It requires members to abolish internal border controls with each other, while strengthening them with non-member states. Its provisions include a common policy on people seeking temporary entry and harmonisation of external border controls. There are cross-border police and judicial co-operation. The area includes all EU states except the UK and Ireland; however, the Schengen Area also includes several countries that are not members of the EU: Norway and Iceland are members stemming from the Nordic Passport Union, which pre-dated Schengen; Switzerland joined in 2008 and Liechtenstein in 2011; and there are no border controls with the three micro-states of Monaco, San Marino and the Vatican City.

The UK did not join because, as an island, it argued that frontier controls were a better way to control illegal immigration than identity cards, residence permits and registration with the police, which apply in other countries. And Ireland is also outside the area because, since its independence from the UK in 1922, both countries have maintained a common passport-free travel area. How well the control of illegal immigration argument stands up in the light of the UK's experience is perhaps open to question; but, if joining the area involved introduction of identity cards, that is something that the UK, having abandoned a scheme to introduce them, would certainly continue to resist.

If Scotland became independent, it would argue that, like Ireland, it was part of a common passport-free travel area with the rest of the UK, with which it also has a unified labour market. It would seem quite unreasonable for a derogation to be resisted when it has been given to the UK and Ireland. But, in the unlikely event that it became a problem, Scotland would then, if it joined the EU, have to install border controls on travel to and from England, a prospect that would alarm many people.

Joining the Euro

Under the Copenhagen criteria, which define whether a country is eligible to join the European Union, membership pre-supposes the candidate country's ability to take on all the obligations of membership, which include adherence to the aims of economic and monetary union (EMU). This would include stating an intention to eventually adopt the euro. However, before joining the euro, a state's legislation, for example in relation to its central bank, has to be compatible with EMU and it must also have achieved a high degree of sustainable convergence, as measured by four specified criteria:

- achievement of a high degree of price stability, with a rate of inflation close to that of the three best performing countries;
- a deficit on the government's budget at or less than 3 per cent of GDP and a debt ratio of less than 60 per cent of GDP or declining so that it is seen to be approaching that level;
- ability to keep to the normal exchange rate fluctuation margins of the European Monetary System (EMS) of which it would have to have been a member for two years;
- durability of convergence within the EMS, as shown by long-term interest rate levels.

There was a fair amount of fudging of these criteria when the eurozone was set up. Several countries, notably Italy and Belgium, did not meet the 60 per cent debt rule but were accepted because they argued that the ratio was falling. Some also had difficulty with the 3 per cent deficit criterion but argued that they had taken action that would enable them to meet it. Greece would not have been admitted if the true state of its finances had been understood.

If independence is achieved as a result of the 2014 referendum, Scotland clearly would not qualify then or, indeed, for some time. The budget deficit would have to be substantially less than its present level – estimated by the Scottish Government at 8.1 per cent for 2010–11 and 5.0 per cent for 2011–12 (including North Sea revenues – see Chapter 1) and its debt ratio, depending on how it is apportioned with the rest of the UK, will certainly be over 60 per cent. It could be argued, of course, that most of the existing members of EMU have debt ratios of more than 60 per cent as a result of the financial crisis and recession. But the UK does not belong to the European Monetary System. Scotland, therefore, would not qualify until it had been a member for two years, had at least shown convincing progress in meeting the deficit and debt criteria, had kept to the normal exchange rate fluctuation margins of the EMS and had proved durability of convergence as reflected in the long-term interest rate on its bonds.

No country can be forced or obliged to join the EMS system of managed exchange rates. When Sweden held a referendum, the result was against joining EMU. It has, therefore, not joined EMS. So long as this position is maintained it will not become a member of the eurozone, although it must have been expected that it would, in due course, when it signed its treaty of accession. No one can now force it to join against the expressed wish of its people, and to ask it to leave the EU in consequence of this would be absurd. The Czech Republic continues to use its own currency, although Slovakia, from which it separated before joining the EU, has joined the eurozone. As a result of the serious crisis affecting the zone over the last few years, it is probably now less likely that the Czech Republic will join EMU in the foreseeable future, although again it must have been expected to do so when it joined the EU.

To my mind, the most important point is that the financial crisis, especially the extreme difficulties experienced by the southern European countries and by Ireland, should have changed perceptions considerably, whatever previous expectations and requirements may have been. Not only will this have made countries that are not yet in the euro-zone less likely to want to join, but also, as they wrestle with the problems of the zone and work towards closer financial integration, including a banking union, the countries now in the zone certainly ought to be less enthusiastic about admitting a newcomer, especially one like Scotland, where its two large banks have so catastrophically had to be rescued.

However, if Scotland became a member of the EU as a new state, it might be necessary to give some sort of assurance about membership of EMU as a long-term objective, after the necessary conditions were met. If so, extreme caution would be necessary. The Scottish Government could insist that this would require a referendum, as took place in Sweden. To join EMU in anything like present conditions, and so long as there was any danger that Scotland could not match the low inflation rates of other members, notably Germany, could be disastrous.

If an independent Scotland were to remain in monetary union with the rest of the UK, in accordance with present SNP Government policy, that would, in any case, preclude Scotland joining EMU, unless the UK did so. That now seems a very distant prospect, if it is a prospect at all. For all these reasons, I would not expect existing members to insist on Scotland adopting the euro as its currency if it seeks membership of the EU as a separate state. In the midst of the present major crisis, the long-term outlook for monetary union in Europe is not at all clear. But circumstances can easily change. My own view, as discussed in Chapter 2, is that Scotland, as an independent country, should eventually have its own currency and this could be pegged either to sterling or to the euro (in the same way as the Danish krone), depending on what seemed in the country's best interest.

An EU Banking Union

The UK, along with Sweden and the Czech Republic, has also opted not to participate in the proposed EU banking union, of which all other EU states (not only those in the eurozone) are expected to be members. So that could become an issue, too. All of this is still at a very early stage, but the participating countries will be required to hand over supervision of their banks to a European Banking Authority under the control of the European Central Bank. This is to be followed by a common means for winding up financial institutions in trouble and a financial backstop for dealing with a banking crisis. These latter arrangements are not yet agreed, but they follow logically from common supervision of the banks.

An independent Scotland would have to decide what it should do about this. If it retained sterling as its currency, it could not reasonably participate in the banking union, so long as the rest of the UK did not do so. But, if Scotland had its own currency, there could be a strong case for it participating, even if it did not join the eurozone, as it would give added protection in the event of a major crisis, such as has been experienced in the last few years.

Conclusion on Opt-Outs

So the EU countries would be faced with something they have never faced before – a country which has separated from a member state, which does not intend to join the Schengen Area or the eurozone, but intends to remain in

monetary union with the rest of the member state from
which it separated. How would that be regarded?

Some other member states, worried about the precedent
it sets for parts of their own territories that might want to
split off and follow the Scottish example, might try to use
negotiations over these derogations as an excuse to raise
difficulties over Scottish membership. Apart from Spain,
where there has been pressure from Catalonia for an independence referendum (despite this being excluded by Article 2 of the Spanish constitution), there is ongoing concern about a possible split in Belgium between Flanders
and Wallonia; and there is also concern in Cyprus that the
northern Turkish part might seek EU membership in its
own right. It may seem unfair, if Scotland otherwise satisfies the criteria, but these other cases are relevant because
they could affect the attitude of other EU governments to
Scotland's position.

The most likely opposition would probably come from
Spain, where the Spanish Prime Minister has recently said
that a country seceding from a member state would be considered to be outside the EU and would have to apply for
membership afresh. But he has held back from saying that
Spain would exercise a veto and his country would have
something to lose, notably access to the Scottish Atlantic
waters for its fishing fleet, if Scotland were excluded. The
last French president also promised that his country would
have a referendum before there was any further enlarge-
ment of the EU. But it could be argued, if necessary, that
this would not apply, since Scotland is already in the EU as
part of the UK. The position, however, remains unclear and
much skilful negotiation might be needed.

These negotiations would involve the rest of the UK
as well, as the secession of Scotland would affect various
aspects of its membership, such as voting rights and the

number of members of the EU Parliament. But if it were accepted that treaty amendment was the course to be followed, such negotiations might be completed quite speedily, perhaps even within two years from the referendum. Scotland might have to agree to some conditions that it did not particularly like but that would become clear in negotiation. Goodwill would be the key to success. It is, therefore, a political rather than a legal issue.

However, it is conceivable that, if relations between the UK and other member states were to deteriorate further, as a result of the present UK Government's desire to renegotiate the terms of its membership, with the threat of an In/Out referendum, the atmosphere of negotiations as regards the future position of Scotland might be quite different. Other member states might then be anxious to retain Scotland as a member, particularly if Scotland indicated its willingness to accept all existing rules and commitments.

The EU Rebate

The rebate was negotiated as a result of extreme pressure from Mrs Thatcher, when Prime Minister, because it appeared that the UK, under the rules that then applied, would contribute a disproportionate share of the revenue for the EU budget and far more than it would get back in payments. At that time, the greatest part of the budget, some 80 per cent, was spent on the Common Agricultural Policy and much of the revenue came from import duties, including on imported agricultural goods. Britain had a relatively small but efficient agriculture that did not qualify for large amounts of support but was a large food importer, especially from the Commonwealth. Since then, however, the EU budget has expanded; agricultural and other natural resource-based support, including a small amount on fishing, is still the largest component of its expenditure but, at 48 per cent in 2011, is much less important than it was, and the structural funds for support to areas in need of development have become a second very important area of spending, amounting to 36 per cent of the total budget.

On the revenue side, the bulk of the money now comes from a contribution based on gross national income (GNI).* In 2012, this is forecast to contribute 74 per cent of total revenue and the proportion has been steadily increasing, probably to ensure that the costs are not too high for the poorer countries.[3] There is also a VAT contribution, which has steadily reduced as the GNI contribution has increased – it now amounts to only 11 per cent of the total. This is probably because VAT is recognised to be much more regressive than a contribution based on GNI, which more accurately reflects what a country can afford. The traditional own resources, principally from import duties, amount to 15 per cent. The contribution of each country is, therefore, more closely related to ability to pay than it was at the time Britain's rebate was started. There are nine countries that contribute more to the EU budget than they get back in receipts (see Table 1). The remaining 18 countries are net beneficiaries. These are the poorer countries, especially those in the eastern part of the EU – Poland, for example, is a major beneficiary – but including Spain, Portugal and Greece. They contribute less, because their incomes are lower, but they are also major recipients, because of the importance to them of agriculture and their need for development.

---

* GNI is net of income paid and received from abroad. This is important as it would certainly be lower than GDP, if GDP included Scotland's geographical share of the North Sea and the profits of all overseas companies operating both offshore and onshore in Scotland.

Table 1

Net Contributors to the EU Budget in 2011

	Gross Contribution million euros	Net Contribution million euros	Cost per head in euros
Denmark	2,448.3	975.2	174
Germany	23,127.1	10,994.1	134
France	19,612.2	6,449.9	99
Italy	16,078.0	6,492.1	107
Netherlands	5,868.9	3,804.6	228
Austria	2,688.7	812.9	97
Finland	1,955.2	662.2	123
Sweden	3,333.6	1,576.6	166
UK	13,825.0	7,255.2	115
UK without rebate	17,420.0	10,850.9	172

Source: European Commission, EU Budget 2011:
Financial Report, *Brussels 2012*

Many countries consider the British rebate no longer justified, especially as Britain is one of the wealthiest countries in the EU. In 2005, it was reduced by 25 per cent but, in future budgetary negotiations, it can be expected that there will be pressure from other countries to end it altogether. Indeed, they might use the occasion of a negotiation with Scotland to try to end it for not just Scotland but also the UK. It would, after all, be reasonable at least to adjust it for the remainder of the UK to take account of Scotland's secession. The amount of each country's net contribution varies by a surprising amount from year to year. According to the EU budget, in 2011 the UK rebate was 3.5 billion euros and, as the table shows, the gross contribution, allowing for the rebate, made by the UK was 13.8 billion euros.[4] This was less than the contribution made by France – 19.6 billion euros – or Italy – 16.1 billion – countries with similar populations. Germany, with a larger population, makes the largest contribution – 23.1 billion euros. After receipts, the net figure for the UK is 7.3 billion euros – still less than Germany but more than the other countries. However, on a per head basis, the table shows that the UK contribution is now substantially less than that of the Netherlands, Denmark, Sweden, Finland or Germany. Without the rebate of 3.6 billion euros, the contribution, less receipts, in 2011 would have been 10.9 billion euros – still slightly less than Germany – and, on a per head basis, without the rebate, this would still be less than Denmark or the Netherlands and only slightly more than Sweden.

Scotland would, therefore, find it very difficult to get a share of the rebate, if it was negotiating to become a member state of the EU in its own right. First, because the other countries would see the negotiations as an opportunity to end the rebate for at least part of what had been the UK. But second, the case for the rebate would be less strong than for other parts of the UK. Scotland has had substantial support from the European Structural Funds for areas scheduled under regional policy. In addition, Scotland has a large agricultural area and much of it is classified as Less Favoured Area under the Common Agricultural Policy (CAP), which qualifies for special assistance; it, therefore, receives a significant amount of support, though perhaps not as much as it should. The Royal Society of Edinburgh's *Inquiry into the Future of Scotland's Hills and Islands*, which I chaired, found that Scotland's receipts from the CAP, especially the amount received for environmental projects, was the lowest in the EU per hectare, and lower than we thought justified. This appeared to be mainly because the UK was anxious to restrain growth in the total EU budget.[5] Perhaps this could be subject to negotiation in future. But, in view of what it would qualify to receive and the attitude of other member states, any notion that Scotland might be able to retain a share of the UK rebate must be dismissed. Scotland would be a net contributor because we know that Scotland would be among the wealthier countries of the EU. But the net contribution per head, even without a rebate, would be unlikely to be as high as for some other small countries, such as Denmark and Sweden and probably Finland.

Membership of the European Economic Area as an Alternative to the EU

As discussed earlier, if Scotland had problems negotiating membership of the EU, it seems more likely that this would be for political than legal reasons. But, if that were to happen or if the conditions attached to membership proved unacceptable, how serious a setback would this be? The Scottish Government has not said it has a plan B for this.

If full membership of the EU was blocked, Scotland could apply for membership of the European Free Trade Area (EFTA), which would give it membership of the European Economic Area (EEA). The EEA countries have unrestricted access to the European single market but have to meet the rules of that market, just as EU members do, and also make contributions to the EU budget. Members of the EEA include Norway, Liechtenstein and Iceland.* Switzerland is not a member of the EEA but has bilateral free trade arrangements with the EU. The main difference between being a full member of the EU and being in the

---

* Iceland has applied for full membership of the EU. But, in view of the importance to it of its fishing industry and its experience in the financial crisis, there are important issues to be considered.

EEA is that EEA countries have no representatives on the EU Commission or Council and no members of the European Parliament; they, therefore, have no influence on the policies of the EU, although they are subject to them and to all the single market rules in order to get unrestricted access to the market. This disadvantage has been a major factor in encouraging countries such as Sweden, Finland and Austria, which were previously members of EFTA, to become full EU members.

A major difference between the EU and the EEA countries is that the Common Agricultural and Fisheries Policies do not apply to the EEA. This has been a significant factor in the decision of the Norwegian public to reject EU membership twice in referenda. Fishing is an important industry for Norway, which, although sharing part of the North Sea with EU states, also has its own continental shelf. Its agriculture faces major handicaps of climate and topography and is, therefore, more highly protected than it would be under the CAP. These considerations, especially for fishing, are also relevant to Iceland. Exclusion from the CAP would mean that Scotland would have to finance all of its agricultural support itself, and such support would certainly be needed, especially in the hill areas and the islands, if agriculture was to remain viable there.[6]

Exclusion from the Common Fisheries Policy (CFP) might seem more attractive to many people, as it is commonly asserted that the policy has been too centralised, generally unsatisfactory for Scotland, and has led to depletion of fish stocks. But the main problem with the fisheries policy is that the efficiency of modern fishing boats has steadily increased to the point at which their ability to catch fish greatly outstrips the supply of fish in the sea.[7] This is what has caused stocks to become seriously depleted. In an attempt to restrain overfishing, the EU has imposed catch quotas. But, in each year's negotiations at Brussels, Ministers (including Scottish Ministers) are pressed by their country's fishing industries, concerned understandably about their livelihoods, to get the best deal they can. This has meant that the quotas have usually been higher than the scientific advice recommends.

Because many people in Scotland regard the CFP as a wasteful failure, there are those who would like to see responsibility repatriated. It is sometimes suggested that this should be one of the subjects in the Prime Minister's proposed renegotiation of the UK's relationship with the EU. The policy certainly needs to become less centralised and some moves to achieve that have already been implemented.[8] It has recently been announced that the practice of discards, whereby substantial quantities of fish are discarded at sea because they are over the allowed quota, is to end. This is welcome and long overdue.

The main difficulty in getting progress over reform is that not all of the fishing nations agree on what should be done. The North Sea, by its nature and geography, is a shared resource between all of the countries with a coastline bordering it. That is how the CFP operates and each country has a quota. If there were not a common policy, major problems would arise if each country tried to operate its own exclusive zone. Fish do not respect international boundaries, so that, to avoid overfishing, some means of limiting the amount of fish caught would have to be applied to all countries sharing that resource. Negotiations to achieve this would be complex and difficult, and it is by no means clear that any resulting policy would serve Scotland better.

What if the UK Leaves the EU?

Overhanging any discussion of Scotland's future in the EU is, of course, uncertainty about the position of the whole UK.

Prime Minister David Cameron has said that, if re-elected, he would intend to renegotiate the terms of UK membership during the next UK Parliament and then put the issue to the country in an In/Out referendum on Britain's membership. Judging by the attitude of many Conservative backbenchers, the more right-wing press and some of the polls, the whole country could be heading towards the exit. The UK's constant ambivalence in its attitude to the EU is trying the patience of other member states and they might not now do much to resist the UK's departure. This does not bode well for a good outcome in a renegotiation.

There can be no doubt, however, that the way in which the EU is operating at present is unsatisfactory. Much of this is the result of extending institutions that were originally designed for six member countries to the enlarged EU of 28. Decisions take too long and are often very difficult, as has been very obvious during the eurozone crisis. Much of the irritation with the EU in Britain, however, stems from the rules for the single market, which seem to many people excessively bureaucratic; this is ironic because the single market has been strongly supported by British governments of both parties. Indeed, the 1992 Programme as part of the European Single Act was the brainchild of a British EU Commissioner, Lord Cockfield. It requires rules on common standards, which can often be complicated, if member countries are to freely admit each other's goods. Otherwise non-tariff barriers, such as differing safety standards, could be a major obstacle to trade.

Whether it is true, as is commonly asserted, that Scotland is less euro-sceptic than England, is not really clear. Some polls have given results that appear to support this and certainly neither the Conservative party nor even less UKIP have strong support in Scotland. As a result of our history, there probably is less concern about sovereignty in

Scotland, which lost much of its sovereignty in 1707, than in England, where it is a relatively new concept. But whether this would result in Scotland voting one way in an In/Out referendum and England the other is far from certain. I suspect that, if such a referendum is eventually held, the disadvantages of leaving the EU and losing influence over so many policies that affect us would become much clearer and may well result in a decision by the UK to continue membership.

The EU will inevitably change, however, if the members of the eurozone proceed down the path of much closer fiscal and political integration, as seems at present to be the intention. Whether formally recognised or not, that would lead to a two-tier EU, with the members of the eurozone forming an inner core and the other countries, of which the UK is likely to be one, in an outer free-trading periphery. Some of the countries not presently in the euro might aspire to join, but equally some of those at present using the single currency might, in the end, decide that the degree of integration envisaged involves a greater loss of sovereignty than they can accept and leave to join the periphery. Recognition of a proper two-tier EU is perhaps inevitable in the end and might make it easier for it to operate effectively, as suggested in some of the proposals for reform.[9]

If Scotland became independent and was accepted as a member of the EU, I would expect it to remain outside the eurozone, for all the reasons already discussed, so that it would be in the outer tier, if there were one. It would not be sensible to try to become a member of the eurozone so long as it was unclear whether inflation in Scotland could be kept at a rate that was compatible with other countries, especially Germany. Failure to do this would result in the economy becoming increasingly uncompetitive; it is because this has happened to several of its members that the euro-zone is in its present difficulties. It must also be doubtful if Scotland, having become independent, would want to sur-render the amount of sovereignty that would be expected of a member of the eurozone.

The really interesting question is what Scotland's atti-tude might be if the rest of the UK voted in a referendum to leave the EU, but Scotland's population voted to stay in. If there is a UK referendum, it will not be before the next UK Parliament and therefore it will be after the Scottish referendum. Scotland's decision will, therefore, have been made. But, if, in advance of the Scottish referendum, it seemed likely that the UK was going to leave the EU, that could become a factor in the referendum debate. Contin-ued full membership of the EU is, in my view, of major importance to Scotland and I would expect this to be the view of business as well, since it guarantees access to the large European market without tariffs or non-tariff bar-riers, that might impede trade; it has also been a crucial factor in attracting international companies to establish themselves here. It needs to be remembered that there is competition between countries for this investment, and Scotland's main competitor is the Republic of Ireland, which would not be slow to take advantage.

Many of those who regard continued EU membership as important and in the best interests of Scotland and its econ-omy might then be more likely to favour independence. A second Scottish referendum, if there is a majority in the UK European referendum to leave the EU, is probably unlikely. But if the result were damaging to Scotland, as I would ex-pect it to be, that could result in serious tension between the Scottish and UK governments. Much might depend on whether the UK still had full access to the European single market. If Scotland left the UK in such circumstances, the disruption caused could still be damaging, especially to the financial sector. But Scotland could also gain international investment, some of which could be at the expense of the rest of the UK, if it was the only part of the former UK in the EU.

Could an Independent Scotland Have Handled the Failure of the Banks?

The bank crisis of 2008 has done immense damage to the British economy and the consequences have been long lasting. At the time of writing, we are still struggling with its effects and, although at last there seems to be a recovery in economic growth, it looks as if it will be some time yet before the legacy of debt is overcome. This chapter discusses why the Scottish banks failed so badly that they had to be rescued, what this implies for banks in future if Scotland becomes independent, and also the implications for Scotland's financial sector, which employs around 100,000 people and is one of the most important parts of the economy.

It was particularly distressing to those of us living in Scotland that it was the Royal Bank of Scotland and Halifax Bank of Scotland (HBOS) which were in the worst state and had to be bailed out by the government. The Royal Bank is a Scottish bank with its headquarters in Edinburgh. It was founded in the 18th century – partly, it is said, because of concern that the Bank of Scotland was too sympathetic to the Jacobite cause. The Bank of Scotland dated from 1695 – before the Act of Union – and had a very proud history. It was the oldest bank in Britain, apart from the Bank of England, which was one year older. As an independent bank, it had enjoyed a reputation for good, cautious management and strong growth, but in 2001 it merged with the Halifax, the largest of the former building societies, to form HBOS. Although technically a merger rather than a takeover, the Halifax was by far the larger partner and most of the combined management team, including the chief executive, James Crosby, and his successor, Andy Hornby, were from the Halifax. The Bank of Scotland had secured agreement, however, that the headquarters of the combined bank would be on the Mound in Edinburgh.

What happened at the Royal Bank would seem to be mainly due to megalomania on the part of the chief executive, Fred Goodwin, who dominated the management team. The directors too must share some of the blame. The bank had mounted a successful takeover of the much larger English bank NatWest, outgunning a rival bid from the Bank of Scotland, which had started the process. The takeover of NatWest was a success and had been well conducted so that it yielded considerable savings. The bank had also extended its business worldwide, with takeovers in other countries, and built a huge new head office at Gogar on the outskirts of Edinburgh. It should have stopped there. It had quite enough to digest and, had it done so, it might not have had to be rescued – or at least it would not have required the amount of help that was eventually necessary.

But in October 2007, with a recession in the offing, together with Santander and Fortis, it launched a joint bid for the Dutch bank ABN AMRO, the largest-ever bank takeover. This was a disaster for both the Royal Bank and Fortis. ABN AMRO proved to be toxic, with many bad loans that would never be repaid; and a key component, desired by the Royal Bank, was removed from the transaction before the sale. Coupled with the onset of the recession and the problems of excessive lending that affected almost all banks, the Royal Bank had engaged in unduly aggressive and high-risk organic growth. The chief executive had pressed for balance sheet growth and the commercial, corporate and investment banking teams were given incentives to deliver this. This pressure for growth, and the incentives to achieve it, resulted in some bad deals rather than careful assessment of risk. All of this brought the bank to the point of insolvency, so that it had to be rescued with a £40 billion injection of taxpayers' money from the government. So the Royal Bank, which had briefly been the largest bank in the world, with outstanding loans exceeding not just the Scottish but the UK GDP by 40 per cent, became semi-nationalised. The government injected capital by taking a 60 per cent shareholding, which later had to be raised to 80 per cent, when more funds were required.

The Bank of Scotland's merger with the Halifax in 2001 came about for two reasons, which are well explained in Ray Perman's recent book.[1] The bank could claim to have had the most successful record of all British banks, both in terms of growth and return on shares, but following financial globalisation and the free-for-all climate that was the product of the Conservative Government's 'Big Bang' in the 1980s, which ended the previous regulatory restrictions, it felt vulnerable to takeover because of its relatively small size. Maybe it was less of a takeover target than it imagined, as it would have been hard for any other management to run it better or to generate substantial savings. But it felt that to survive it had to grow. The problem was that, although it could increase the size of its loan book, it could not get its deposit base to grow sufficiently to support it, without having to rely on wholesale finance from elsewhere in the sector. Originally banks had based all of their lending on their deposits. And, had they continued to do that, there would have been no banking crisis. But the Big Bang in Britain and the repeal of the Glass-Steagall Act in the United States enabled retail banks to move into investment activities that had hitherto been the province of merchant banks in Britain or investment banks in the United States. This was not a feature of the Bank of Scotland or HBOS. It was a much riskier activity, but potentially also much more profitable than retail banking, and it made takeovers in the banking sector much easier and more likely – hence the threat felt by the Bank of Scotland management.

To help the bank to grow, without being too dependent on wholesale finance, the Bank of Scotland first attempted a merger with the former building society Abbey National. This proved abortive when it was impossible to agree terms. The irony is that, had the bank only waited, it could have taken over the Abbey National with a hostile bid on its own terms, as it was not long before the latter got into trouble. Instead, Abbey was taken over by Santander.

Having failed in its bid for NatWest, and also in its attempted merger with the Abbey National, the bank felt that it had become exposed and that the chances of it itself becoming the subject of a takeover had increased. Accordingly, when the possibility of merger with the Halifax arose, it seemed attractive. The Halifax had demutualised to become a bank. It had a huge mortgage book, with about a third of the total mortgages in the UK, and it seemed to the Bank of Scotland to offer a deposit base on which profitable lending could be increased.

Looking back, with the benefit of hindsight, at what happened to the world's banking sector in the period before 2008, some of what was done then seems hard to credit. How could institutions, whose credibility was based on their sound judgement in handling people's money, have got into such a mess? But, as with previous financial bubbles, few people saw it coming or had any understanding of the danger they were in. The securitisation of mortgages, whereby lenders, instead of keeping outstanding mortgages on their books as assets, had been able to divide them, package them and sell them on the world market as bonds, had made possible a huge housing boom. There was, however, a fatal flaw – once a mortgage had been securitised and sold, the original lender no longer needed to be concerned about the borrower's ability to meet the interest cost or eventually to repay the loan. This is what probably led mortgage companies to extend their lending to people in the United States who would never be able to pay – the so-called 'subprime' mortgages. In the UK, too, banks – the extreme example being Northern Rock – and also some building societies began to lend recklessly, sometimes agreeing to a loan of a value even higher than that of the underlying asset, let alone what that asset – a house or a flat – might be worth in a falling market. Banks also began to accept self-certification of income from mortgage applicants. People with self-certified mortgages that had been inadequately checked or with loans with a value that was higher than that of the asset on which they were based, would be in serious trouble if they became unemployed or if interest rates rose.

The original lender became even more removed from worry about the ability to pay interest or redeem their loans when these securities were further sliced, diced and repackaged to form 'collateralised debt obligations' (CDOs). CDOs could themselves be further subdivided and repackaged into what were called 'CDOs squared'. By the time all this repackaging and subdividing had taken place, the risk on such bonds was widely spread. This was hailed by many people as an advantage, since any risk was well diluted and spread; but the fact was that few people understood the nature of these securities and no one dealing in them was able to assess the degree of risk they contained. Indeed, Robert Peston, in his excellent book *How Do We Fix This Mess?*, says that to assess the risk involved in all the mortgages that were contained in a CDO squared would take a diligent person seven years of constant reading, if one assumes that there were 150 mortgages in every CDO involving a prospectus of 200 pages, and 300 pages in every prospectus for a CDO squared.[2] Even the ratings agencies – Moody's, Fitch, and Standard & Poor's – could not do this. They seem to have been taken in by those who claimed that risk was negligible because it was so widely spread. Amazingly, they gave triple-A ratings, the highest available, to these securities.

The banks used these securitised assets to augment their deposits as a base for their lending; and, because they were so highly rated, they did not have to be covered with a substantial amount of capital, when it came to satisfying the international requirements for capital adequacy set out in the Basel agreements at the Bank for International Settlements. This is what led to disaster. It never seems to have occurred to those responsible that, at some point, these assets might not be able to be sold or might be sold only at a heavily depreciated price. Once the markets realised that many of these securitised assets were toxic, their value plummeted and they became impossible to sell. While the Bank of Scotland had seen attractions in the merger with the Halifax, because it offered the prospect of increased lending using the large Halifax deposits as a base, the new management of the merged bank went much further. The emphasis was not on assessing risk but on selling more and more loans. It sold their mortgages as securitised assets and extended lending far beyond the deposit base. Lending was very profitable, so it was encouraged, not only by expanding what was already the largest mortgage book of any of the UK lenders but especially by increasing lending in the commercial loan sector where Peter Cummings was in charge. He was a Bank of Scotland rather than a Halifax man, but, encouraged by senior management, he excelled in increasing commercial lending.[3] The inevitable result was that, when the whole-sale market dried up, HBOS became spectacularly insolvent and had to be rescued in a rushed merger with Lloyds TSB, in which the Government took a 43 per cent shareholding. When, in 2009, it became apparent that the HBOS losses were much larger than previously thought, the Government announced that it would increase its stake in Lloyds Bank-ing Group to 65 per cent.

After the crash, Cummings was severely criticised by the Financial Services Authority (FSA), disqualified from work-ing in banking and made to pay a fine of £500,000. He would argue that it was successive chief executives, James Crosby and Andy Hornby, both of whom were from the Halifax, who pressed him to increase lending by so much. It may be a mistake to lay all the blame on Cummings, as many would argue that he would not have been able to do what he did if the old Bank of Scotland management had been in control.

What Could an Independent Scotland Have Done?

There are those who will argue that a Scottish government and a Scottish regulator would never have allowed the Scottish banks to get into such an overextended state. Well, maybe. But the Scottish First Minister was encouraging Fred Goodwin, chief executive of the Royal Bank, a bank in which he himself had once worked, right up to the last. And being independent and having their own regulator did not stop Ireland, Iceland or Spain from getting into a similar mess. So a Scottish regulator would have had to have been endowed with better foresight than any of its counterparts in these other countries. The fact is that almost no one fore-saw the crisis developing in the way that it did.

Assuming that the RBS takeover of NatWest and the Bank of Scotland's merger with the Halifax had taken place, the crisis would obviously have required intensive discussions between an independent Scottish government and the government of the remainder of the UK to agree a joint plan. The rescue of Fortis in the three Benelux countries is sometimes quoted as an example of the sort of rescue that would have had to take place. Fortis was a conglomerate – its banking operations included both commercial and investment banking, but it also had a substantial insurance business. It was split up after the catastrophic attempt to take over ABN AMRO. The Dutch Government nationalised the banking and insurance subsidiaries in the Netherlands. The Dutch banking business was then renamed ABN AMRO and the insurance business was split off as ASR Nederland. The Belgian part of the banking business was sold to the French bank BNP Paribas. The rest of the insurance business, which was substantial in Belgium, remained with Fortis, but its name was changed to Ageas.

Discussions between the governments were far from easy, involving a good deal of argument to get a fair division of the assets, and this led to several attempts by shareholders to take legal action before the deal was finally settled. A Scottish government would have had to have been involved in similar discussions with the government of the remainder of the UK and there would have been room for much disagreement, especially over the division of assets abroad. Probably the Scottish parts of HBOS (the old Bank of Scotland) and the Royal Bank would have had to have been nationalised at considerable cost to the Scottish taxpayer, leaving the government of the rest of the UK to deal, in whatever way it chose, with the parts of the two banks in England and Wales. International subsidiaries would probably have been put up for sale.

Whether an independent Scotland was able to maintain some form of monetary or currency union with sterling, as the SNP Government has stated to be its policy and, if so, whether UK financial institutions retained any role for regulation in Scotland is unknown. It is therefore not helpful to speculate.

However, there are some points that can be made. If there was a separate Scottish bank regulator – and that would seem to be a requirement for a member state of the EU, as well as being a commitment in the Scottish Government's white paper[4] – responsibility for the activities of the Scottish banks and indemnification of any losses made by depositors would be in accordance with whatever Scottish bank insurance scheme was operated and ultimately with the Scottish Government. But, if the operations of Scottish banks in England and Wales were carried out through subsidiary companies rather than merely branches, these subsidiaries would have to be subject to the regulator for the rest of the UK. Compensation of depositors in these subsidiaries would then be the responsibility of the insurance scheme operated in the rest of the UK and would ultimately lie with the UK Government.

This became an issue with the collapse of the Icelandic banks Glitnir, Landsbanki and Kaupthing, which had expanded recklessly during the boom years to the point where their combined debt exceeded by six times the annual output of Iceland's economy.[5] The depositors' insurance scheme for Iceland's banks gave protection up to 20,000 euros, but it was inadequately funded to meet the costs of compensation when the banks collapsed. Icelandic depositors were compensated, but those with deposits in Icesave, an online branch of Landsbanki operating outside Iceland, were not. The British and Dutch governments decided to fully protect retail depositors with accounts in

Icesave and then tried to reclaim from Iceland the cost that the Icelandic insurance scheme should have covered. This amounted to 3.9 billion euros, which was close to 50 per cent of Iceland's reduced GDP. To impose such a burden on Icelandic taxpayers, especially when the Icelandic population was less than that of the city of Edinburgh, was clearly unaffordable. A deal was proposed that involved payment over 15 years at an interest rate of 5.5 per cent. This was rejected by Iceland's population in a referendum. One can imagine that there would be a similar reaction from the Scottish population if they had been asked to meet the costs of compensating English and Welsh deposit holders of Scottish banks operating in the rest of the UK after they had recklessly expanded.

Iceland has been accused, before the EFTA Surveillance Authority, of not meeting the requirements of a European Economic Area directive aimed at ensuring that bank deposits were properly covered by insurance; it has also been accused of discrimination because Icelandic depositors were compensated but those abroad were not.

Kaupthing bank, however, owned the UK bank Singer & Friedlander as a subsidiary company. No claim could have been made on Icelandic taxpayers for compensation in this case, since it was regulated by the UK authorities and any compensation required was a charge met by the UK insurance scheme.

What would have happened had Scotland been independent at the time of the banking crisis would, therefore, have depended on how the banks were organised and regulated at the time. Had NatWest and the Halifax been set up as subsidiary companies for which the regulating authority was for the rest of the UK, there would have been a charge on the UK bank insurance scheme and no liability on the Scottish scheme or on Scottish taxpayers. But, had there been branches in England of the Scottish banks, the same liability would have arisen as affected Iceland. The Scottish insurance scheme would have had to pay and, if that was inadequate, there would have been recourse to the Scottish Government and ultimately to Scottish taxpayers.

Compensating depositors of failed banks, however, is not the only issue. As what has happened in Ireland demonstrates, the banks have other major obligations and costs. If a bank fails, the shareholders stand to lose their money, but what about those who hold bank debt in the form of bonds? In the global financial market, these bonds are held very widely across the world by other banks or by institutions such as pension funds. The Irish Government guaranteed all these liabilities; it is said, in fact, that they were pressed to do so by the European Commission because of the knock-on effects on banks and institutions such as pension funds all across Europe if they did not do so.[6] But it proved a major mistake. Bonds, after all, should not be regarded as risk-free – that is why the interest on bank and company bonds is higher than on gilt-edged securities. To have simply allowed the banks to go bankrupt would have caused a lot of people to lose money, but it would probably have been preferable for Ireland. The cost of meeting the banks' liabilities was much higher than the Irish Government had estimated and it overwhelmed Irish state finances. Although Ireland's government had been in a strong financial position, with a surplus on its budget before the crisis and its debt in relation to GDP one of the lowest in Europe, the guarantee of the banks' liabilities imposed such a heavy burden that the government had to seek a bailout from the IMF, the European Central Bank and the European Union.

I believe, had Scotland been an independent state in 2008, it would not have been able to cope with the losses incurred by its banks, whatever arrangements had been put in place. Even if the banks and the Scottish authorities had had the foresight to ensure that operations outside Scotland were conducted by subsidiaries regulated in those countries, they would have had to face the same problems as Ireland. Indeed, none of the Irish banks were on the scale of the Royal Bank or HBOS. If this had happened – and I think it would have – the Scottish Government's finances would have been overwhelmed and, like Ireland, it would have had to seek a bailout from international organisations.

Lessons for the Future

But what is past is past. What is important now are the lessons to be learnt for the future. Clearly, other countries have to learn lessons, too. One obvious lesson is that it is dangerous for banks to grow so large in a small country that they cannot be supported if they fail. Another is that normal retail banking should not be put at risk by investment activities that, however profitable, could jeopardise the viability of the bank.

The UK Government set up the Vickers Commission to recommend action that needs to be taken. It has suggested increased levels of capital to support lending so that banks have a larger cushion against insolvency. This is clearly important and welcome. The commission also recommended ring-fencing the investment activities of banks to keep them separate from retail banking.[7] Others, including the Parliamentary Commission on Banking Standards, chaired by Andrew Tyrie, have questioned whether this goes far enough. It appears that they would like to see the ring-fence 'electrified' and the legislation to contain a reserve power for complete separation. The intention is that investment or 'casino' banking should be sufficiently separate so that it could not put ordinary retail banking at risk and, if necessary, be allowed to fail in a crisis. A large combined bank cannot be allowed to fail because of the dire consequences for the whole economy. In that situation, investment bankers get huge bonuses if they do well but, if they do badly, there is an unwritten guarantee from the government that they will not be allowed to fail. My own view coincides with that of the Parliamentary Commission – that the Vickers' recommendation, despite being unpopular with the banks, does not go far enough.

Scotland has a substantial financial sector, employing approximately 100,000 people. This includes not only the banks but also life assurance companies, such as Standard Life and Scottish Widows, fund managers, investment trusts and many professionals such as stockbrokers and financial advisers. Some have their base in Scotland; others have their head offices elsewhere in the UK but have major businesses in Scotland. The growth of the sector has been partly responsible, along with North Sea-related businesses and other international and domestic investment, for Scotland's GDP per head being higher than for all the other countries and regions of the UK, apart from London and the south-east of England. Its future is, therefore, of the greatest importance to employment and income in Scotland.

The Scottish banks are the centrepiece of the financial sector and were one of the features that made the country distinctive. They have been a source of much pride in the past. That is why the failure of the two large banks was so keenly felt. The first lesson must be that there are grave dangers in having banks that have so clearly outgrown the size the economy, as was evident in Iceland. Many people take the view that Britain's banking sector, even against the size of the UK economy, is too large, to the point at which it poses a risk. So, if Scotland becomes independent, it should aim at having a banking sector that will not overwhelm the economy if things go wrong.

There also needs to be much tighter control of credit. As Robert Peston shows, after the banks started using mortgage-backed securities to increase their lending, they reached a point where there was a shortage of borrowers – banks were more or less throwing loans at people, accepting self-certification for mortgages, as well as offering mortgages at very high loan-to-value ratios.[8] Credit was rising at a much faster rate than the growth of the economy, whereas, before the Big Bang, it had risen at approximately the same rate. So long as it lasted, lending was highly profitable. Now the situation is in reverse, as the banks try to rebuild their balance sheets.

The Connection between the Banks and Housing Policy

An aspect of this that has not yet been sufficiently addressed but which, in my view, is very important is the connection between lending and housing policy. It is no accident that in the UK, Ireland and Spain (all countries that got into serious difficulty) the proportion of homeownership in the housing stock was extremely high. It is now about 65 per cent in the UK (having fallen from 70 per cent in 2004) and, although it used to be much lower in Scotland, the gap has almost disappeared, with owner occupation now about 64 per cent of the total stock. In Germany, on the other hand, less than half of the housing stock is in owner-occupation and it is even lower in Switzerland. In France, it is not much over 50 per cent.

In Britain, since the 1980s, homeownership has been strongly encouraged by the government, and Right-to-Buy on heavily discounted terms has resulted in tenants buying much of the local-authority stock. This policy has had the effect of transferring wealth to the less well-off in society. The result has been a remarkable housing boom, which was made possible by the great expansion of bank lending. This long-lasting boom led to a tripling of house prices in the decade and a half up to the peak in 2007. People came to expect house prices to always rise, and to rise faster than inflation or earnings; but it had not always been so. At the end of the 1980s, there was a sharp drop in house prices for several years. But that was forgotten. People came to think that a house was an investment in which one could not lose, that it was worth taking out a huge mortgage to provide funds for other things, such as an expensive holiday or luxuries of various kinds, because, with house prices going up, there would never be any difficulty in paying it off.

Ownership is the preferred form of tenure for most people in Britain. But it is dangerous if people are encouraged to take on the burden of ownership when they cannot really afford it, or will be unable to afford it if interest rates rise, as inevitably they do from time to time. Despite interest rates being very low following the crisis, many owners were in difficulty with their mortgages. Some are still paying interest only, having stopped the element of repayment. Others have difficulty even with the interest. The threat of possible repossession causes a lot of pain and anguish. Other countries have a much larger, properly regulated rented sector – some of it social rented from housing associations and some of it privately rented.[9] The costs of the former are set below commercial rents, with an element of subsidy; the latter is market-determined. In both cases, the landlord takes responsibility for maintenance, which can involve major unexpected costs that an owner-occupier in financial difficulty could find it hard to afford. For those on low incomes in rented accommodation, whether they are in work or unemployed, disabled with little or no income, or those who have fallen on really hard times, housing benefit is available.

It is a feature of any modern society that there is a section of the population that cannot afford homes of a standard that society considers acceptable. In the old days that led to slums, which were in time replaced by council housing. The experience of Europe, especially Scandinavia, but now also Scotland, seems to show that social housing can be best provided through housing associations. But there also needs to be a strong private rented sector of good standard for people who may have to move often or who do not yet feel able financially to take on the responsibilities of ownership.

Much of the excessive lending by banks is connected with housing debt. It is no kindness to encourage people who cannot afford it into homeownership. It causes hardship for the people concerned and ultimately, when there are defaults, serious damage to the lenders, with consequences for the whole economy. I therefore welcome the Scottish Government's decision to end Right-to-Buy. That policy played its part at a time when there was too much reliance on local authority housing. But the future of housing policy in Scotland now needs a proper reappraisal to provide a better balance between ownership, private renting and social renting. It has to be recognised that the drive to homeownership was responsible, to a large extent, for the excessive lending that caused the financial crisis, as well as a great deal of pain for individuals who were stretched beyond their means. Any thinking on the future of banking in Scotland, therefore, needs to be coupled with a housing policy reappraisal to provide the population with a good quality of housing without the pain of individuals being stretched beyond what they can afford and without the financial sector taking risks that cause acute pain for individuals and jeopardise the prosperity of the country.

Conclusion

So, an independent Scotland would have to think hard about its banks, its housing policy and its financial sector. What size should the banks be? How should they be regulated? How, if they have activities in other countries, should they be structured so as not to cause an insupportable burden, should they fail?

Independence would probably cause the Royal Bank of Scotland to move its headquarters to London, where it might trade as NatWest, in recognition of the fact that the bulk of its customers were in England. (It would be odd after Scottish independence to retain the name Royal Bank of Scotland for a bank headquartered in London.) For its Scottish banking activities, it would probably trade through a subsidiary, which might retain the name of Royal Bank of Scotland. Lloyds Banking Group has its headquarters in London, although the registered office is at the Mound in Edinburgh. It would probably transfer its registered office to London and constitute Bank of Scotland as its subsidiary company for its operations in Scotland. Losing the headquarters operation of the Royal Bank would be a blow for Scotland and for employment, but such a structure would be in the best interest of an independent Scotland, since it would save the Scottish people from being called on to carry the potential burden of businesses that were too big for them to support in a crisis.

The Scottish Government's intention was to set up a Scottish regulator that would work together with a shared sterling area regulatory authority. It also proposed a shared compensation scheme that would apply to depositors. That now seems unlikely to be acceptable to the Government of the rest of the UK. If Scotland set up its own central bank, however, as well as its own regulatory authority, there would then also have to be a separate Scottish insurance scheme for depositors.

For the rest of the financial sector, many of these same issues apply. Many of them – Standard Life and Scottish Widows, for example – have more customers in the rest of the UK than in Scotland. Might they also decide to move their headquarters to where the majority of their clients are, either to London or some other city south of the border? The fund managers, such as Aberdeen Asset Management, Baillie Gifford and Martin Currie, also have the bulk of their clients in England. Might they too think of moving? That might depend for all of them on whether full monetary union continued. The potential loss to Scotland's financial sector, which has been one of the strongest parts of the economy and very important for both income and employment, could in this case be substantial. The SNP Government have sought in the white paper to give an assurance that, because there would be full monetary union, these dangers would not arise. But this must remain one of the principal risks that could follow independence.

It will be objected that cities such as Luxembourg and Zurich have substantial financial sectors and that there is no reason, therefore, why the Scottish financial sector needs to be affected. But the financial sectors in these cities are very different from those in Scotland. What needs to be recognised is that, if having the bulk of their clients outside Scotland means that a business would do better in England, it will move. The implications are very large. The financial sector is of major importance to Scotland; it is a part of the economy that has grown enormously and is one of the country's strengths. It is essential that it should continue to prosper whether or not there is independence. The Government, therefore, needs to give much thought to how its future can be best secured and, as a matter of urgency, it needs to open up discussions with the firms concerned.

Scotland's Energy Future

Under the Scotland Act of 1998 energy policy is a reserved matter for the UK Government, but the Scottish Government has responsibility for planning decisions. This means that it could refuse permission for new developments, such as a nuclear power station, and that planning decisions for developments such as wind farms, though initially for local government, rest ultimately with Scottish Ministers. They also have responsibility for an agreed proportion of electricity to be generated from renewable sources under the Renewables Obligation (Scotland). This division of responsibility may appear unsatisfactory and is probably not understood by many people but appears to have worked quite well. Certainly the Scottish Government has developed its own view on energy policy and, as planning decisions are involved in most aspects of development, such as wind farms or sites for hydraulic fracturing ('fracking') to produce gas or oil, it is right for them to do so.

In the summer of 2011, there was a debate in Edinburgh organised by *The Spectator*. The subject was 'Scotland's energy policy is just hot air'. There were speakers for and against this motion, but a large majority at the end of the debate supported the motion. There were many who criticised the Scottish Government's policy, but little was said about the responsibility of UK Ministers. What was particularly evident in the debate was concern – and, indeed, hostility – about the effect of the widespread development of wind farms on Scotland's landscape. It also seemed that there was a good deal of scepticism about climate change.

My own view on climate change is quite simple. I am not a climate scientist, but I respect the overwhelming view of those experts who study the subject. This is that climate change is real and that, although there have been major changes in climate over a long period, the only plausible factor that can account for the changes that have been observed over the last century or so is the increased release of greenhouse gases caused by human activity. Apart from changes in temperature, it is also predicted that there will be more extreme weather events and certainly experience of recent years seems to bear that out.

In a major report published in 2006, the Scottish Environment Protection Agency (SEPA) found that, since 1961, there had been significant changes in Scotland's weather – Scotland had become much wetter.[1] Although there have been large variations from year to year, there has also been an increase in average winter precipitation of 60 per cent in the north and west, and an average annual increase for the whole country of 20 per cent. Some parts of north-west Scotland have become up to 45 per cent drier in summer. The average period of snow cover has decreased over 40 years as a result of milder autumn and spring temperatures. The sea level around Scotland has risen and the seas have warmed by one degree Celsius over the last 20 years, causing changes in the abundance and distribution of marine species. A successor to this report has not been published, but the findings of other studies confirm the changes that are taking place, and SEPA has published its own climate change plan.[2]

There are still quite a number of climate change deniers. But, whether one accepts the findings or not – and I do – the issue is of such importance and the consequences potentially so serious that it would be foolish to do nothing. Lord Nicholas Stern in his important review for the Government argued that, while policies to try to halt climate change were expensive, the consequences of doing nothing could be catastrophic for the world and would cost a great deal more.[3]

I, therefore, welcome the Scottish Government's targets for replacing dependence on fossil fuels with renewable forms of energy. These targets have been revised and are ambitious. At a conference in Glasgow in October 2012, the First Minister said that it was now intended to have 50 per cent of Scotland's electricity demand supplied from renewables by 2015. He felt it was possible to achieve this because Scotland had met 35 per cent of demand from renewables in 2011, as against a target for that year of 31 per cent. The aim is now to meet the equivalent of 100 per cent of Scotland's electricity demand from renewable sources by 2020, and the Scottish Parliament has passed legislation requiring greenhouse gas emissions to be cut by 42 per cent by the same date. These targets are clearly very ambitious, but producing the *equivalent* of 100 per cent of Scotland's electricity demand would not mean that there will be no demand for electricity from other sources. Some of Scotland's electricity output is likely to be exported, as it is now; and renewable energy is variable in its availability, so that other sources of power will always be needed as back-up.

Scotland is well endowed with a wide variety of energy sources. Coal production provided the energy for the Industrial Revolution in the 18th and 19th centuries. At its peak, the output of coal was over 20 million tonnes a year, but it is the most carbon-emitting form of energy and all of the deep mines in Scotland are now closed. However, a considerable amount of coal – some 5 or 6 million tonnes a year – is still produced from opencast workings and is used in Scottish power stations.[4] North Sea oil and gas are both now past their peak production and are expected to continue to decline, but the output is still substantial, as we will see in Chapter 7. Imports to the UK from other sources are now growing and, in the case of gas, now account for about half of the supplies in the UK; but the output of both from the North Sea still greatly exceeds Scotland's requirements and will remain significant for at least another generation.

The Royal Society of Edinburgh in its major *Inquiry into Energy Issues for Scotland* found that 34 per cent of total energy was required for domestic use, some 28 per cent for transport, 21 per cent for industry and 16 per cent for services.[5]

Electricity Generation

About a quarter of energy used in Scotland is required to make electricity but, as Table 1 shows, a substantial 23 per cent of the electricity output is exported through the interconnector to England and a further 3.5 per cent to Northern Ireland. So Scotland is a major exporter of electricity, with more than a quarter of its output going to other parts of the UK. In 2011, 33 per cent of Scotland's electricity was generated by nuclear power, 21 per cent by coal, 15.7 per cent by gas, 26.8 per cent by renewables, 2.3 per cent by oil and the remainder, a very small amount, from burning waste.[6]

Most of the electricity produced is now generated in four large power stations with a combined capacity of 7,229 megawatts (MW): one coal-fired – Longannet; two nuclear – Hunterston B and Torness; and one gas-fired at Peterhead (see Table 2). Most of these are now quite old, the most recent being Torness, which was commissioned in 1988. Cockenzie, a coal-fired power station that had a capacity

Table 1

Scottish Electricity Generation and Use 2011

	GWH	percentage
Coal	10,779	21.0
Gas	8,052	15.7
Oil	1,156	2.3
Nuclear	16,892	33.0
Hydro	5,936	10.4
Wind, wave and solar	6,992	13.7
Other renewables	1,404	2.7
Waste	12	1.2
Gross Total Supply	**51,223**	100
Pumped storage and own use by major generators	-2,924	5.7
Own use by other generators	-353	0.6
Transmission and distribution losses	-2,444	4.8
Net total supply	**45,502**	88.8
Exports to England	-11,597	22.6
Exports to Ireland	-1,769	3.5
Supplied to Scottish consumers	32,136	67.5

Source: Department of Energy and Climate Change, Energy Trends, *December 2012*

of 1,200 MW, no longer met EU emission standards and closed in March 2013, but it may get a new lease of life if Scottish Power's plans for a new gas-fired plant on the site are implemented. If it proves practical to produce gas from shale in Scotland, this could encourage the implementation

Table 2

Electricity Generating Capacity (Main Producers) 2011

	Capacity in MW
Coal	
Longannet	2,400
Cockenzie	1,200
Gas	
Peterhead	2,177
Nuclear	
Hunterston B	1,288
Torness	1,364
Hydro	
Natural flow	1,489
Pumped storage	720
Wind and wave	3,016
Other renewables*	305
Total renewables**	4,810

*landfill gas, sewage gas, other bioenergy
**excluding pumped storage
Note: Figures are for maximum capacity which will be greater than capacity available at any one time.

Source: Department of Energy and Climate Change, Energy Trends, December 2012

of these plans. The largest plant, Longannet, is more than 30 years old, but it has been upgraded with flue gas desulphurisation scrubbers to reduce emissions of SO_2 and NOx, the gasses responsible for acid rain; it has also been adapted to enable gas to replace 20 per cent of the coal and will burn environmental waste composed of heat-treated dried sewage sludge. Hunterston B has just had its life extended to 2023, while Torness can also be expected to have its life extended in due course. Peterhead, which was re-powered with increased capacity in 2000, is now to have a refit to lengthen its life and increase its flexibility. It should, therefore, have considerable life left, too. So it is likely that, one way or another, and in contrast to what was expected till recently, all five plants (if a rebuilt Cockenzie goes ahead) could remain operational for many years yet.

In 2011, there was 5,685 MW of capacity in renewable power stations, an increase of 1,042 MW or 22 per cent on the previous year. But this capacity is not available all the time – it depends on the amount of water for hydro and wind for wind farms. The hydro stations, since they were first developed, have been a major economic benefit to Scotland. Unlike the renewables now being developed, they have not required subsidy. They are individually much smaller than the five large fossil-fired and nuclear stations, ranging from just a few megawatts to over 100 MW. Combined, they have a considerable capacity, but many of them have insufficient water resource to run their turbines all the time and are designed to store up the water to use it to run their turbines to meet peak demand. For this, they are extremely valuable, particularly in complementing the nuclear stations, which are base-load stations that cannot readily be turned off and on. The fossil-fired stations are more flexible than nuclear, especially Peterhead, which burns gas. A coal-fired station takes some hours to start up, but gas-fired stations can be started up at shorter notice, though not as quickly as hydro power. Demand for electricity is highly variable, depending on time of day, time of year and temperatures. Moreover, a key feature of electricity is that it cannot easily be stored, so that there has to be capacity to meet the highest expected peak demand. The flexibility of the hydro stations is, therefore, of great benefit to the whole system.

To the natural flow hydro stations, most of which date from the 1940s and 1950s, has recently been added the large Glendoe plant, with a capacity of 100 MW. In addition to these are the two pumped storage schemes at Cruachan and Foyers, with a combined output of 700 MW and an ability to store the equivalent of 1,510 MW in the form of their water resource. These do not add to the total supply but use off-peak electricity to replenish their reservoirs so that they are available to generate at full power during peak periods. Scottish and Southern Energy have announced plans for two more pumped storage schemes, one in the Great Glen at Loch Lochy, near Spean Bridge, and the other at Invermoriston. Together, these will add a further 900 MW of capacity.

No power station has a 100 per cent load factor. There have been major and sometimes prolonged outages at the nuclear plants and even the fossil-fired stations have to have their boilers shut down for maintenance. But, in the renewable sector, the load factor is much lower. The Scottish hydro stations have a load factor of about 45 per cent, simply because there is not sufficient water in the reservoirs to run the turbines all the time. But this is manageable. Installed capacity is deliberately more than can be run full time. Its output can, therefore, be planned and although rainfall varies, there is enough in Scotland, especially in winter, to generate as much power as is required to match demand.

Wind power is much less predictable. The load factor for onshore wind in Scotland in 2011 was 27.4 per cent, only marginally better than in England. For offshore wind, it was higher, 35.8 per cent, but, as yet, there are relatively few offshore wind farms. Very often, when the weather is coldest in winter, an anticyclone over the country means there is very little wind. This, coupled with the major impact that wind farms have on the landscape and the subsidy that is still required, has led a lot of people to question the value of investment in wind energy. It means, too, that other forms of energy have to be available as back-up; that requires investment in plants that may be only intermittently required.

In the meantime, there are further substantial developments planned for wind farms. If the aim were to replace the two nuclear stations with wind farms as they come to the end of their lives, a great deal of additional capacity would be required. Although the present wind and wave capacity (3,016 MW) is theoretically greater than that of the two nuclear stations (2,653 MW), with a load factor of only 27 per cent, it would be far from enough. Just to match the annual output of the nuclear stations something like a tripling or quadrupling of wind capacity would be needed. It is claimed that Scotland has the potential for 11,500 MW of onshore wind farm capacity, and even more, about double this amount, offshore, where the load factor is better but the cost is higher. But these figures for potential capacity take no account of the intermittent nature of the supply. Obviously a lot of Scotland would be covered with wind farms and the present hostility to them would, understandably, become very much more intense. There is also concern about their effect on tourism because of their effect on the landscape. These worries may well be justified and they could become much more serious if there is a huge amount of additional development. There would then be strong pressure on politicians and local planning authorities to oppose it.

In my view, it is essential, if wind farm development is to be acceptable, that local communities receive some benefits from it. The small development of three turbines by the island community of Gigha is an interesting example of how this can be done. The proposed scheme by Viking Energy, a joint venture of Scottish and Southern Energy and the Shetland Charitable Trust, is another. This large development of 103 turbines, with a capacity of 370 MW, now has planning permission to go ahead, although its opponents tried to use legal action to stop it and are still active.

The advantage of this project is that Shetland has far more wind than mainland Scotland, as demonstrated by the existing small Burradale wind farm, which has a load factor averaging 52 per cent. The output of Viking Energy would be far in excess of Shetland's needs and the intention would be to export it by cable to the mainland. Such a cable, however, would itself be an ambitious project, considering the substantial distance involved, and would be a challenge both to finance and build. Nevertheless, it is estimated that the Shetland Charitable Trust could get an income from its investment in Viking Energy of over £20 million a year, dwarfing even the substantial income the islands get from North Sea oil.

There are ways in which the variability of supply can be mitigated. The hydro stations can complement wind power, as already mentioned, and the additional pump storage schemes to be built by Scottish and Southern Energy will add considerably to this flexibility, making power available when required and when the output from wind is low. There is scope for some further hydroelectric development and certainly for considerably more pump storage capacity if needed.[7] Other forms of renewable energy may in time also help to mitigate the peaks and troughs of wind energy.

A great deal of work is being done on the development of wave and tidal energy – especially in Orkney, where the tidal flow in the Pentland Firth is exceptionally strong. Tidal energy in particular, although intermittent, is regular and therefore much more predictable than wind energy. But, although these projects offer promise for the future and the resource is reckoned to be considerable, the technology is in its infancy and it will be many years yet before it is able to be used commercially. The pioneering PURE project in Shetland, which uses two small wind turbines to make hydrogen, could also be a way of storing energy when it is not required and making it available when it is. Manufacturing hydrogen from wind power is also of interest when providing energy in more remote areas, where costs of linking to the grid are high; the Western Isles Council aims to follow the example of Iceland in using hydrogen to power its public transport.

But perhaps the best way to tackle the intermittency of wind power is by extending the grid, on the principle that the wind will always be blowing somewhere – in Shetland, Orkney or the Western Isles, if not on the Scottish mainland. It is with this in mind that the First Minister has had discussions in Norway about an undersea cable linking the two countries. The major obstacle with this would probably be the cost, but it is worth investigating further. Already, in addition to the grid interconnectors linking Scotland to England and Ireland, England is linked to the Continent, from which it is a net importer.

The Viking Energy project in Shetland, if it goes ahead, will test the viability and cost of a long undersea cable. The company's assessment indicates that the cost would not destroy the viability of their project. There has also been a recent report of a proposal to run a cable from Iceland to the Scottish mainland to deliver geothermal electricity, which is abundant and cheap, from Iceland's volcanoes.[8] Apparently, this was considered some years ago and rejected on the grounds of cost. It would require a cable of 1,000 kilometres, the longest sea cable in the world, and would go through much deeper water than the cable from Shetland, but Landsvirkjun, the Icelandic electricity producer, believes that it may now be viable. If it went ahead, it could

118   SCOTTISH INDEPENDENCE

provide a valuable means of balancing any irregularity in production from Scotland's renewable energy.

These proposals highlight the importance of access to the grid at reasonable cost. There has been much complaint about this, with renewable power sources in the north and west of Scotland being expected to pay much more for a connection than power sources nearer the market in the south of England. This is, of course, an economic matter – absence of long distribution lines involves less cost to the grid and means that power sources nearest to the market would expect to pay less than those furthest away, especially if there is a shortage of power in the south and a surplus in the north. But the cost of connection to the grid could make some of the best renewable sources of power uneconomic to develop. This, therefore, needs to be subjected to rigorous scrutiny to ensure that these costs are reasonable and can be justified.

The report by the Royal Society of Edinburgh, *Inquiry into Energy Issues for Scotland*, argued for a mixture of electricity suppliers, so as not to be too reliant on one source, bearing in mind all the uncertainties. A proposal from Scottish Power for an experimental carbon capture plant at the Longannet coal-fired station was rejected by the UK Government on grounds of cost; but a proposed carbon capture and storage (CCS) plant by Shell and Scottish and Southern Energy linked to the Peterhead gas-fired power station has been selected by the UK Government for funding, along with a proposal for the Drax coal-fired station in Yorkshire. A proposal from a consortium at Grangemouth was also on the shortlist but, although considered an excellent bid, was not selected. These plants would inject carbon into oil or gas fields in the North Sea. If the technology succeeds, it would provide a way of making emission-free energy from fossil fuels, which could be very important for the future. But, even if it is successful, the costs for the foreseeable future are likely to be high.

By the time Scotland becomes independent, if it does, onshore wind power could be virtually economic without subsidy. Bloomberg New Energy Finance has forecast that onshore wind power will be economic by the second half of this decade, as a result of economies of scale and improvements in technology. This accords with the view given by various experts in evidence to the House of Commons Select Committee on Energy and Climate Change.[9] Unlike nuclear power, where costs have remained very high, wind power has got progressively cheaper as the efficiency of turbines has improved and the benefits of scale production are realised. But much will depend on how prices change for other forms of energy, an issue I touch on later.

Offshore wind generally causes people (with the exception of Donald Trump) less environmental concern over its visual impact and has a better load factor, but is, at present, much more expensive. Here, too, costs are likely to come down in time, as technology develops, but for the foreseeable future investment in offshore wind is unlikely without significant subsidy.

The subsidy for wind power is provided through Renewables Obligation Certificates (ROCs) and the Climate Change Levy. These require the power companies to meet targets for the generation of renewable energy but, inevitably, that puts up the cost of the electricity supply, which has to be met by consumers. Since Scotland has much more wind power than either England or Wales, it follows that consumers in England and Wales are meeting part of the subsidy for wind energy in Scotland. This is an important issue for the independence debate. A Scottish government might find that English and Welsh consumers were unwilling to subsidise Scottish wind power electricity, if Scotland

120 SCOTTISH INDEPENDENCE

were a separate country. This, however, would depend on whether the rest of the UK was able to meet its renewable energy targets by some other means or, despite the requirements of clean energy, decided to ignore them.

The response to this is usually that England and Wales will still want electricity exports from Scotland. But, if their own supplies of electricity cannot cover their needs, they would seek the cheapest supplies available. This might still be electricity from Scotland but, if they thought that too expensive, they would have the option of additional investment in England and Wales or of importing supplies through the interconnectors with the Continent or from Ireland, where large wind farm developments are planned specifically for exporting power. According to the Irish, they will be capable of generating far more electricity from wind power than their country needs. The Irish Energy Minister, Pat Rabbitte, and the UK Minister, Ed Davey, have recently signed an agreement to work together on renewable energy.

So the future for energy supplies in Scotland has plenty of promise. Scotland undoubtedly has exceptional renewable resources and the technology will continue to develop. There would seem to be two main dangers. The first is a public backlash if the view strengthens that ever-increasing wind farm development is damaging the landscape – though it is fair to say that it is much easier to decommission a wind farm after 25 years than to decommission a coal-fired station, let alone a nuclear plant. The second is that, because it is expensive, the wider market for Scotland's renewable power resources may not materialise as hoped. Grid connections may prove too costly to finance, cheaper power may be available from elsewhere or heavy investment in English shale gas may remove the pressing need for additional electricity from renewable sources.

The 'Fracking' Question

Already the hydraulic fracturing revolution, known as 'fracking', has resulted in a huge drop in gas prices in the United States, where they are now only about a third of the price of gas in Europe. It is difficult to overstate the importance of the change that has resulted in the United States from this development. There is now the prospect that the United States will not only be self-sufficient in oil and gas supplies but will also become a major exporter. Indeed, the International Energy Agency has forecast that the United States will overtake Saudi Arabia in oil production by 2020.[10] If so, this will certainly affect the international oil price. Gas markets have so far been much more local, since gas is less easily transported. But there is a growing international trade in gas, resulting from the development of large gas-carrying ships. And it is significant that the plans of Ineos at Grangemouth, which were announced following the strike that nearly closed the plant in the autumn of 2013, include the importation of large quantities of gas from the United States.

Gas is a cleaner form of energy than coal, releasing only about half the amount of CO_2 for the same amount of energy released. But it is still, of course, a fossil fuel. If it were developed in place of clean energy, it would not enable Britain to meet its carbon reduction targets. But it is cheap and would probably be the cheapest form of energy generation. Its use in place of coal would bring down the UK's carbon emissions substantially and many people see it as a useful bridging fuel, until more renewable power is developed. It is also well suited as back-up for renewable power, where the output is variable.

But the development of fracking could, through bringing down energy prices, make it more difficult to produce electricity economically from Scotland's renewable sources. This could obstruct investment in new renewable capacity, although projects already built would presumably continue to generate electricity, since the marginal cost of wind power is close to zero.

The scale of gas supplies from fracking in Britain, or indeed Europe, is of course still largely speculative. The potential is thought to be much less in Europe than the United States, but geology suggests significant suitable rock in Poland and the UK, notably in north-west England, the English Midlands and Sussex.[11] The British Geological Survey has estimated that there may be 1,300 trillion cubic feet of shale gas present in the north of England. This is not the amount that can be extracted, but it indicates a very substantial resource. Even if only a small fraction is recovered, it could still be very large, given that, in the peak year of 1999, output of gas from the North Sea was enough to supply the whole UK at 4 trillion cubic feet. There are also significant amounts of suitable shale rock in the Central Belt of Scotland and in the North Sea off the Scottish coast[12], where existing installations for offshore oil or gas fields might reduce the infrastructure cost of exploiting these reserves.

The exploration company Cuadrilla Resources has drilled three wells in Lancashire, in the Bowland Basin, and is drilling a fourth. It is expected that it may start fracturing in 2014. In evidence to the House of Commons Select Committee on Energy and Climate Change, the company said that it estimates the resource of the Bowland Basin as very substantial.[13] Cuadrilla says that the resources in Lancashire come from shale more than a mile thick, which is probably unique and is thicker than the shale being exploited in the United States.

At present, the uncertainties surrounding shale gas are

probably similar to those affecting North Sea oil on its discovery; it would be wrong, therefore, to put much weight on any of the estimates.

There has been much concern from environmentalists about these developments, notably the possible effect on water and wildlife, and there have been two very minor earth tremors in Lancashire. Only time will tell if these are serious concerns or if they will be overcome with appropriate regulation and following the recommendations set out in a joint report by the Royal Society and the Royal Academy of Engineering, as the proponents of fracking claim.[14]

The UK Coalition Government has now given its support to shale gas development, but so far the Scottish Government has failed to do so, possibly because the Green Party, its partners in the referendum campaign, are opposed to the development. In my view, this is short-sighted and unfortunate. If shale gas in the United States is having such a big effect in lowering costs for industry, especially for chemical manufacture, there is a real danger that competition will result in a loss of jobs in Europe. The plan to import shale gas to Grangemouth may save a plant that would otherwise have had an uncertain future, so why not develop the industry here on our own doorstep? Moreover, the development of shale gas in Scotland, if investigation proves it viable, could be the best way of ensuring that energy-using industries in Scotland remain competitive against international competition.

As for the effect on climate change, there must be real uncertainty about Scotland being able to meet all its energy requirements from renewables in the foreseeable future, even if, as hoped, they play an increasingly large part in supply. The Cockenzie coal-fired power station has already closed and the Scottish Government has said that it will not approve a new nuclear power plant to replace the two existing power stations. They both have at least ten years' life left but replacement has to be planned many years in advance; although not emitting carbon, a new nuclear plant would be very expensive. Shale gas, if the developments prove successful, offers a cheap form of energy and a substantial reduction in carbon emissions compared with coal. It makes little sense to import shale gas from the United Sates or to keep encouraging the development of oil and gas in the North Sea, while at the same time failing to exploit shale gas in Scotland. Carbon Capture offers hope that in the future, once the technology has been developed, production of shale gas could be made virtually free of carbon emissions. I, therefore, support the view that it could be attractive not only as a bridging fuel, giving time for a carbon-free energy supply to be developed, but also to provide a back-up for renewable energy supplies.

The main barrier to shale gas development in the UK is the plethora of regulations that apply and a system of planning that can be extremely slow. There is also worry and apprehension from the general public about the environmental impact. Furthermore, the Crown owns the minerals under the soil, whereas in the United States they are owned by the landowner. This means that landowners there see the chance of major financial benefit from fracking; in the UK, communities where development takes place might get no benefit at all, only disturbance. If, therefore, fracking development is to go ahead, there needs to be legislation to simplify the regulations and to improve planning procedures, without in any way relaxing the need for safety or avoidance of damage to the environment; but there also needs to be a clear policy to ensure benefit for local communities by giving them a statutory right to share in the profit.

The importance of all this for energy policy in an independent Scotland is simply to emphasise the uncertainties. At this stage informed opinion seems to think it unlikely for a variety of reasons that gas prices in Europe would fall to anything like the extent seen in the United States: apart from the problems already mentioned, there is likely to be much stronger resistance to development in densely populated parts of Europe, such as Lancashire, than in the sparsely populated areas of the United States where much of the development is taking place. In the UK, the most that seems to be suggested at present is that shale gas might be enough at least to stabilise gas prices and stop dependence on imported gas from increasing further. But in reality it is too soon to assess what the effect on energy prices might be. In Scotland, where there is experience of the shale oil industry, there might be less resistance to development. Moreover, unlike the former shale oil industry, fracking leaves no heaps of spoil on the surface and, with modern drilling techniques, including horizontal drilling, the above-ground impact would be small.

Conclusion

Scotland is very fortunate in its wealth of energy resources. Apart from oil and gas from the North Sea and open-cast coal, it has renewable energy resources of which many countries would be envious. But with the exception of hydropower, these resources all need to be subsidised until either technical progress or rising international energy prices make them commercially viable. The Scottish Government has said it will not be prepared to approve proposals for new nuclear power in Scotland when the two existing nuclear stations come to the end of their lives. This would take 2,600 MW of baseload capacity out of the system.

Significant potential for gas from fracking has been identified in the Central Belt. But this has not yet been subject to assessment with exploratory drilling and, unlike the UK Government, the Scottish Government has so far given no commitment either to the assessment or exploitation of this resource. This, in my view, is most regrettable. It is by no means clear that renewable energy alone will be adequate on its own, cheap enough or sufficiently reliable, for all Scotland's needs, especially as there is growing opposition to wind farms. Gas, although a fossil fuel that releases carbon, releases much less than coal, and it could usefully complement Scotland's renewable energy from wind, where the major problem is reliability.

If the UK is to meet its climate change targets, Scotland's renewable energy resources will still be needed, whether or not fracking develops in the UK as a major domestic source of gas. But subsidy is likely still to be necessary for offshore wind for many years and will certainly be needed for wave and tidal power, which are still only in the very early stages of development. This will impose a burden either on consumers or taxpayers, which, under present arrangements, would fall on the UK as a whole. Complete dependence on renewable energy, because of this and its variability, does not seem convincing as an energy policy for an independent Scotland. If fracking does, contrary to present expectations, bring down energy prices substantially, that would obviously be welcomed by consumers; but it would prolong the need for green sources of energy to be subsidised. It could also affect development in the North Sea, where the fields being exploited will be increasingly costly, either because they are smaller or in deeper water. The important question for Scotland, therefore, if it becomes independent, is whether consumers in the rest of the UK would be willing to continue to pay the necessary subsidy for Scottish green energy.

Might they look for alternative sources of imports, which might be cheaper, or would the drive for lower prices, both to help consumers and enable the economy to compete with other countries, make UK politicians abandon their carbon targets?

North Sea Oil: The Mishandling of an Opportunity

The revenues from North Sea oil and gas have become a major part of the independence debate because economic issues have featured so prominently in the case for independence. As was shown in Chapter 1, Scotland, like the UK as a whole, has had a substantial budget deficit since the banking crisis of 2008 and the ensuing recession. Although the First Minister and others have argued that Scotland's deficit in the last few years has been proportionately less than that of the UK,[1] this has certainly not always been the case and it depends on the assumption that some 90 per cent or so of the oil and gas revenues would accrue to Scotland as an independent country.[2] This is based on the median line, as estimated by Alex Kemp and Linda Stephen of Aberdeen University, both highly respected researchers on oil and gas. But, as I pointed out earlier in the book, there are a fair number of assumptions involved in the First Minister's calculation, which cannot be taken for granted.

The reason this is so important is, as explained earlier, that Scotland has, and has had for many years, a higher level of public expenditure per head than the UK average. An assumed geographical share of the oil and gas revenues in the last few years would approximately compensate for this, though not to the extent of eliminating all of the present deficit. So the issue is whether these revenues can be relied on to continue at this level, or at least until, by some means, the economy can be made more productive, so that non-oil tax revenues are increased.

In 1974, when I was Chief Economic Adviser at the Scottish Office, I wrote a paper for Ministers which was obtained a few years ago under freedom of information. This paper, which sparked some controversy, was written as confidential briefing for Ministers at the time of the 1974 election. I argued that the then outgoing Government in their public statements had underestimated the scale of the developments in the North Sea and that the tax revenues ought, by 1980, to be very large; however, this was dependent on appropriate tax and other policies being put in place by the incoming Government to secure them. I went on to argue that the scale of these revenues made it no longer tenable to say that an independent Scotland could not manage financially. Scotland's economy, at that time, was in a worse condition than it is now, with many of its industries in difficulty.

The paper was intended as something of a wake-up call for both Ministers and their officials, some of whom had not realised the importance of what was happening in the North Sea; and it urged that stronger action, through regional policy and by other means, was needed to help the Scottish economy. Everything I said in the paper turned out to be right about the scale of the development and of the revenues; indeed, at £3.7 billion in 1980–81 in the then current prices, they were even somewhat higher than my estimate. But the paper has become rather notorious; it has been claimed it was even suppressed. That was not the case. Confidential briefing for Ministers is never published and, had I published it on my own initiative, I would have been breaking all the rules that apply to civil servants and would have been in serious trouble. Furthermore, I did not think that what I was saying was so earth shattering. The paper was based on information mostly from public sources and at least one newspaper was making the same arguments.[3]

But that was 1974, and the situation was different then. Gas was already flowing to England from the southern basin of the North Sea and the network was being extended to Scotland. But oil production from the northern North Sea did not start until 1975 and only became substantial from 1980 (see Graphs 1 and 2). The big hikes in international oil prices, first in the mid-1970s and again in 1979, meant that, when oil production grew in the 1980s, the revenues generated for the Government were very large indeed, especially in the early part of the decade before the sharp fall in international oil prices after 1984. Oil prices have risen again from their low point in the 1990s and, in recent years, have been very high (Graph 3). Gas prices are much less volatile: although gas is increasingly being traded internationally, the greater difficulty in transporting it means that, whereas the oil market is international, the gas price depends much more on local markets.

Graph 1
UK Crude Oil Production

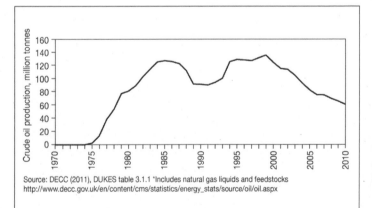

Source: DECC (2011), DUKES table 3.1.1 *Includes natural gas liquids and feedstocks
http://www.decc.gov.uk/en/content/cms/statistics/energy_stats/source/oil/oil.aspx

Graph 2
UK Gas Production

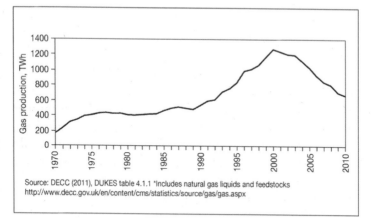

Source: DECC (2011), DUKES table 4.1.1 *Includes natural gas liquids and feedstocks
http://www.decc.gov.uk/en/content/cms/statistics/source/gas/gas.aspx

Graph 3
Crude Oil Prices

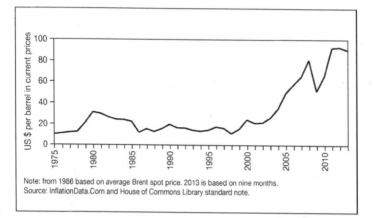

Note: from 1986 based on average Brent spot price. 2013 is based on nine months.
Source: InflationData.Com and House of Commons Library standard note.

Production and Outlook for Offshore Oil and Gas

What matters now is the present position and how it is likely
to develop. Graphs 1 and 2 show that North Sea oil production peaked at 137 million tonnes in 1999, and that offshore gas production peaked at 115 billion cubic metres in
2000. By 2011, crude oil production was down to 52 million
tonnes and offshore gas to 46 billion cubic metres – both
less than half peak output. From 1981 to 2004, exports of
crude oil from the UK had exceeded imports but, by 2011,
exports were only equal to slightly over half the amount imported. That does not mean that offshore oil and gas are un-
important – their life has been extended beyond the original
estimates, as more has been discovered, and is now likely to
last for at least another 30 or 40 years. How much will be
produced and how long it will last depends on what new discoveries are made and on improvements in technology that
enable a higher proportion of the oil and gas to be extracted
from existing wells. Oil & Gas UK announced in April 2013
that production is expected to increase to some 2 billion bar-
rels of oil equivalent* in 2017 compared with 1.5 billion in
2013. This follows a big increase in investment by the oil
companies, notably BP in its Clair Ridge project, a major
field that should be in production until 2050. Nevertheless,
over the long term, the decline in output of both oil and gas
is expected to continue at a gradual rate, despite these developments. Alex Kemp, the official historian of North Sea oil
and gas,[4] said at a recent hearing of the House of Commons
Select Committee on Energy and Climate Change that this
decline might be at a slower rate than in the last few years
and oil output might stabilise for a period, but he did not
expect the decline to be reversed.[5]

* A term used in the industry, 'oil equivalent' means oil plus gas and natural
gas liquids all converted to the equivalent in oil.

Graph 4
North Sea Tax Revenue at Current Prices

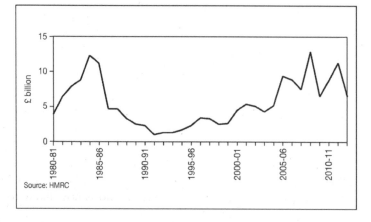

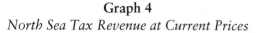

The tax revenues, however, depend on not just the volume of oil and gas produced but also on international oil prices and the profitability of the companies producing the oil. Tax revenue is obtained from both oil and gas, but is much greater from the production of oil because price depends on international rather than local markets. The most obvious feature of oil prices, however, is their volatility. After the high levels of the 1970s and early 1980s, the oil price fell sharply and remained low in the early 1990s. Today, the price is high again, although not as high as a few years ago. Gas production rose steadily to its peak in 2000, and oil production fell after 1985 but rose again thereafter to its peak output in 1999. The consequence of these price movements, coupled with the trends in output, was that tax revenues, which had been very high in the early 1980s, reaching £12 billion in 1984–85, fell to around £1 billion in the early 1990s before rising again to a peak of £12.9 billion in 2008–09 (see Graph 4). This latter peak, though high, is not actually nearly as high in real terms (allowing for inflation)

as it was in 1984–85. If the revenues are recalculated using constant 2009–10 prices, they would have been £28 billion in 1984–85 (see Graph 5).

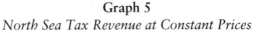

Graph 5
North Sea Tax Revenue at Constant Prices

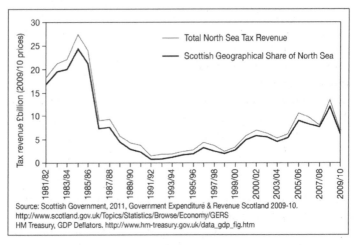

Source: Scottish Government, 2011, Government Expenditure & Revenue Scotland 2009-10.
http://www.scotland.gov.uk/Topics/Statistics/Browse/Economy/GERS
HM Treasury, GDP Deflators. http://www.hm-treasury.gov.uk/data_gdp_fig.htm

What is likely to be the level of tax revenue in future? According to HM Revenue and Customs, oil and gas revenue for the UK as a whole was £11.3 billion in 2011–12 and fell to £6.5 billion in 2012–13.[6] The Scottish Government's forecasts and that of the independent Office for Budget Responsibility (OBR) differ widely, which in view of all the uncertainty is hardly surprising. The OBR has revised its estimate downwards during the last year. There was a sharp fall from £10.6 billion for the Scottish share of UK revenues in 2011–12 to £5.9 billion in 2012–13 and its forecast is for a fall to £3.9 billion in 2017–18, making a total of £27.1 billion over the six years (see Table 1). The Scottish Government has set out various projections depending on different assumptions about output, prices and profits. All of them, however, give substantially higher revenues than the OBR forecast – even the lowest one, which assumes the same level of production as the OBR. If, however, an increase in production is assumed, as projected by Oil & Gas UK, and prices remain at $113 a barrel for oil (the Scottish Government's second estimate), the revenues would be as shown in the second line of Table 1, or £8.5 billion in 2016–17 and £48.1 billion over the five years. If both an increase in output and in prices in real terms are assumed, this gives the Scottish Government's highest estimate of £57.1 billion over the five years, as illustrated in the third line of Table 1. This increase in output is, however, likely to be temporary; all the estimates would show a decline in later years.

Table 1

OBR and Scottish Government Projections of the Scottish Share of North Sea Tax Revenue – £billion

	2012–13	2013–14	2014–15	2015–16	2016–17	2017–18	Total
OBR	5.9	5.0	4.6	4.2	3.5	3.9	27.1
SG (a)	6.9	7.5	8.0	7.9	8.5	9.2	48.1
SG (b)	7.2	8.3	9.4	9.7	10.7	11.8	57.1

NB. SG (a) is the Scottish Government forecast assuming a constant price of $113 a barrel for oil. SG (b) assumes an increase in both output and prices in real terms.

Source: Scottish Government, Scottish Oil and Gas Statistical Bulletin, 2013;
Chancellor of the Exchequer's Autumn Statement, 2013

What is one to make of this? The three projections are based on forecasts of output, prices and profits, all of which are extremely hard to predict. Inevitably, any projection is subject to a wide margin of error. Many people expect oil and gas prices to remain high or to go even higher. This may turn out to be what happens, if China and India continue to develop at the speed of recent years. Since both are such huge countries, demand from them is likely to have a major impact on the market, pushing up prices of many raw materials, including oil. Uncertainty in the Middle East, the world's largest exporting region, is also something that cannot be discounted. On the other hand, oil prices tend to go in cycles. When prices are high, production is increased and energy saving measures are given more priority. This can lead to prices falling, as has usually happened in the past. The fracking revolution referred to in Chapter 6 is a further important factor, as it could lead to prices falling, especially if, as predicted, it makes the United States not only self-sufficient in gas and oil but also an exporter. We have yet to see what impact fracking may have on European markets. All we can really say is that future prices are uncertain.

The revenues from oil and gas also depend on the cost of producing it. As the most productive sources are depleted, it is to be expected that costs will go up. More marginal resources will be brought in to production. Indeed, the large Clair field, west of Shetland, is in water depths of over 500 feet. It is now being developed, although it was earlier thought to be uneconomic. And, if advances in technology enable a higher yield to be obtained from existing wells, that too is likely to be at a cost. So even if the oil price remains high or goes up further, it does not follow that profits and hence tax revenues would remain as high. The inconvenient fact is that they are impossible to predict and attempts to be accurate are only likely to be misleading.

At the House of Commons hearing already referred to, Fergus Ewing, the Minister in the Scottish Government responsible for energy, was asked about decommissioning costs when the rigs and platforms in the North Sea have to be removed. A rough estimate of £30 billion has been mentioned. Professor Kemp had already said that these costs would have to be met by the oil companies when decommissioning started and that they would be a charge against their profits, thereby resulting in lower tax revenue. Mr Ewing, on the other hand, seemed to be arguing that, if Scotland became independent, the rest of the UK should meet part of the decommissioning costs because, for part of their lives, many of these fields had been generating profits and tax revenue for the UK. This would presumably mean that the Scottish Government would expect the Government of the remainder of the UK to pay some compensation for the reduced tax revenues accruing to the Scottish Government after decommissioning starts. This strikes me as a very hard one to sell and one that would be bound to be resisted – especially as both the First Minister and Mr Ewing repeatedly assert that Scotland, with its share of the North Sea, would be one of the wealthiest countries in the world.[7] But, as we have seen in Chapter 1, this is based on GDP per head, which is not a good measure of wealth, as it includes oil company profits received by shareholders, many of whom are not resident in Scotland).

The Case for an Oil Fund

The First Minister has argued for the setting up of an oil fund based on the Norwegian model and has suggested that, if £1 billion was paid into this fund each year, it could be worth £30 billion in 20 years' time. This would, of course, depend on whether it was possible to set aside £1 billion a year, when it would start and what rate of return could be expected. Ministers have tried to clarify the aim, saying that payments would be made into the oil fund as soon as fiscal conditions allow. This is a laudable aim – one that I strongly favour and argued for in a second paper I wrote for Ministers in the 1970s. In that paper, I made two main points: first, that there was a danger of a sharp rise in the UK exchange rate in the 1980s as oil production got under way, thereby replacing imports and making it harder to export; and second, that part of the tax revenue should be paid into a special fund.[8] The Scottish Government's Fiscal Commission has now also argued for a fund.[9] In its report, it recognises that oil revenues are likely to vary considerably from year to year, with the potential to seriously unbalance the Government's budget. It, therefore, sees oil revenues being paid into the fund as a means of providing much needed stability, as well as building up a useful asset.

As Alex Kemp explains in his *Official History of North Sea Oil and Gas*, this was considered seriously in the 1970s.[10] What Ministers in the then Labour Government had in mind, however, was not so much a fund that would accumulate, as the Norwegian fund has done, but a fund to finance capital expenditure, such as key infrastructure projects or the modernisation of industry. This was to include an emphasis on regional development in Scotland, Wales, Northern Ireland and the Development Areas of England. In the end, however, a majority of the Cabinet were against it as being unaffordable at that time. It should be remembered that this was considered in February 1978. The state of the UK economy was extremely difficult, with high inflation and balance of payments difficulties, and North Sea revenues had not yet begun to flow in any substantial quantity.

Although Alex Kemp reports that there was further discussion in the Treasury in the 1980s, the issue does not appear to have been considered by the Conservative Government collectively. Instead, the effect of the oil and gas production on the balance of payments, coupled with the very tight monetary policy being pursued at the time, was indeed to push the exchange rate up dramatically, as I had predicted. The pound, having been trading at $1.60 in the late 1970s, rose to $2.40 in the early 1980s, with catastrophic consequences for much of manufacturing industry, which found it hard to compete with imports or to export at this exchange rate. This was a difficult period for Scotland, which in consequence lost much of its manufacturing industry. Some of this would inevitably have gone anyway, especially the heavy older industries, as it was no longer competitive, even with a favourable exchange rate. But much was lost that might have been retained. Almost all of manufacturing had a difficult time during these years and many firms that did not go out of business contracted sharply. In effect, the tax revenue from the North Sea ended up paying for the resulting unemployment.

The decade of the 1980s was the time when an oil fund should have been set up. If payments had been made into it then, continued in subsequent years and allowed to accumulate like the Norwegian fund*, it would, by now, have been worth a huge amount of money. The Norwegian fund was established in 1990 and receives the state's total cash flow from petroleum activities. It is now the largest wealth fund in Europe, worth some £330 billion, dwarfing the country's national debt and amounting to 70 per cent more than the whole output of the Norwegian economy in one year. The fund is carefully managed, with the revenue being invested abroad rather than in Norway, to counteract the effect it would otherwise have on the balance of payments

---

* This is known as the 'government pension fund – global' – *Statens pensjonsfond – utland*, or SPU.

and exchange rate. Some of the income from these investments is used to finance capital and other projects in Norway, but much of it is reinvested, which accounts for the fund's remarkable growth.

The UK has, of course, a much larger economy, but a fund of this kind would have ensured that there would have been no doubt about the UK's credit in the present economic crisis and it would have saved us much of the misery from the austerity we have been suffering. That such a fund was not set up, when it could have been, was very short-sighted and, in my view, a tragedy. It amounts to a serious mishandling of the greatest economic opportunity the UK has had in the last two decades of the 20th century.

If it becomes independent, would Scotland be right, even now, to try to set up an oil fund? What I take to be the aim of SNP Ministers is something more along the lines of the Norwegian fund than the sort of fund the British Government was considering in the 1970s. Professor Kemp, in his House of Commons committee evidence, said, yes, it would be right, because using the oil revenues to pay for current spending is running down a capital asset, albeit a naturally endowed one, to pay for what should be funded by ordinary tax revenues. The Nobel Prize-winning economist Professor Joseph Stiglitz has said the same.[11] The asset will disappear with nothing to replace it. I agree. It is just that it would be very difficult to do at the moment. If Scotland became independent and the oil revenues were immediately diverted to a special fund, the rest of the budget would be heavily in deficit. That would mean that there would have to be big tax increases or public expenditure cuts on top of what the Coalition Government has already imposed. The Scottish economy would be pushed into an even worse recession and the level of unemployment would rise even further. I do not think that is practical. So I agree with the Scottish Govern-

ment's declared policy of putting the oil revenues into a special fund as soon as fiscal conditions allow. That should not
be taken as a licence to put it off indefinitely, but it may be
a considerable time before reducing the deficit would enable
significant amounts to be set aside.

The Shetland and Orkney Oil Funds

The only parts of the UK with the foresight to set up oil
funds from which they could benefit were the Northern
Isles. Shetland pioneered this arrangement. Under the lead-
ership of its then chief executive, Ian Clark, the council set
up a fund into which oil companies were required to make
a 'disturbance' payment for oil passing through the terminal
at Sullom Voe. It required the oil companies were to share
a properly planned common user terminal, which some
of them had been reluctant to do; and because so much –
probably nearly half – of the oil was in waters for which
Shetland was the nearest landfall, the amount of oil going
through the Sullom Voe terminal was very large indeed. The
proceeds, based on the throughput of oil, have been paid
into the Shetland Charitable Trust, which now has assets in
excess of £210 million and income able to finance expenditure of approximately £11 million a year. Orkney Islands
Council followed the example of Shetland with a smaller
fund based on the oil flowing through its terminal on the
island of Flotta.

Shetland has used its money for a variety of charitable
purposes of benefit to the local community. There are first-
class leisure centres in all the main population settlements,
there is exceptionally good care for the elderly, including
specially built homes and visiting day carers, which reduce
the burden that would otherwise fall on the NHS. There
is investment in property to let and in a district heating

scheme, both of which yield a return. The Trust has also part-funded the excellent Shetland Museum in Lerwick. But perhaps most significant of all will be the investment, along with Scottish and Southern Energy, in Viking Energy's proposals for the large wind farm referred to in the previous chapter. If this goes ahead, it could give further major financial benefit to the islands.

With so much of the oil in Shetland waters, Tavish Scott, the MSP for Shetland, together with Liam McArthur, the MSP for Orkney, has submitted a paper to the UK Government emphasising the distinctive position of the Northern Isles. The islands were incorporated into Scotland by an Act of the Scottish Parliament in 1472, but they have their own separate identity, of which they are very aware, stemming from their Norse heritage.

There are some in London who have suggested that, if Scotland becomes independent, Shetland might prefer to stay as part of the United Kingdom. I have never thought this likely but, as Tavish Scott says, the Shetlanders are in a strong bargaining position if they care to use it. The centralising tendencies of Scottish governments since devolution are not welcomed in the islands, and Shetland is conscious of the advantages its neighbour, the Faroe Islands, have as a dependency of Denmark rather than an integral part of the Danish state. In this respect, they are analogous to the Isle of Man or the Channel islands, which are British dependencies. The Faroe Islands are not part of the European Union, although they have unrestricted trade access to it. This has enabled them to retain control of their own fishing policy, an industry on which the islands heavily depend, and which is also of great importance to Shetland.

Brian Wilson, the former MP and Energy Minister, writing in *The Scotsman*, is well aware of some of the feelings in Shetland and, with his long association with the Western

Isles, has suggested that all three island groups have something to gain from a change to their status.[12] At the time of writing, it would not surprise me if we hear a good deal more of this. As Scotland moves towards the referendum, it would seem right, both for those in favour of independence and for those against, to give some thought to this issue, if indeed there proves to be a demand for change. With so much of the oil in the waters off these islands and their great potential also for renewable energy, it would be a huge mistake not to take the matter seriously, whether Scotland becomes independent or not.

Conclusion

The main point that has emerged from the discussion in this chapter is the great uncertainty surrounding so many of the issues relating to North Sea oil and gas. We know now that the resource is likely to last much longer than was originally thought and to remain important for many years yet. But we also know that output of both oil and gas is less than half of what it was in 1999, the peak year for oil, and in 2000, the peak year for gas. There is now more investment taking place than for some years past and this might result in an increase in production for a while, as the oil companies claim, but thereafter it is expected that the decline will be resumed and continue gradually, maybe for 40 years.

The price of oil in future international markets is very uncertain. There was an expectation that it might continue to rise as a result mainly of rising demand, especially from the Far East and other developing countries, and that may still prove to be right, but the fracking revolution, which is already having a major impact on prices in the United States, could make that less certain.

All that we can be really sure about is that oil prices are

likely to be very volatile, just as they have been in the past. This volatility will affect the taxation revenue that an independent Scotland could expect to receive. Will a rising oil price compensate for a reducing output? This uncertainty could make it very difficult for those who would have to manage the Government's budget. The proposal to set up an oil fund, partly to stabilise the budget but also to accumulate savings, is to be commended, but it would be difficult at present to put any revenue aside without either raising taxes or further cutting public expenditure. It is only realistic to expect that there will be a lot of pressure to use the money for other pressing needs.

As far as the Northern Isles are concerned – the only part of Britain that has been wise enough to set up such a fund – it would be a serious mistake to ignore any aspirations they may have to resist the tendency to increased centralisation or for some change to their status. The islands are of critical importance to Scotland, whether it becomes independent or remains part of the UK, both for their key position in relation to offshore oil and their huge potential for renewable energy.

Welfare and Inequality

Social protection is the largest single programme in Scottish public expenditure, as it is also in the UK. In Scotland in 2011–12, it made up 38.4 per cent of all identifiable public expenditure, at a cost over £21 billion, compared with almost £19 billion for health and education combined (see Table 1).* It includes the state pension and benefit expenditure for the disabled, the unemployed and those with low incomes, as well as Housing Benefit and care for the elderly. Over 70 per cent of this expenditure, some £14 billion, is the responsibility of the UK Department for Work and Pensions (DWP) and is not devolved; rates of state pension and benefits are, therefore, the same throughout the UK. Of the remainder, about £1 billion is paid directly by the Scottish Government and some £5 billion by Scottish local authorities.

Given its huge cost, it is obviously important to consider where the main responsibility for welfare should lie – whether with the UK Parliament, as it does now, or with the Scottish Government and Parliament. Although the Scottish Government's role in social protection is at present limited, much of the expenditure for which Scottish Ministers are responsible is closely related. Health, for example, is a Scottish Government responsibility, as are education and

---

* Identifiable expenditure excludes defence, foreign embassies, interest of the National Debt and other items that are costs for the UK as a whole and cannot be allocated to a particular part of the UK.

skill training, and housing. The Scottish Government pays for Free Personal Care but Attendance Allowance is paid by the DWP. Scottish Ministers in the present Government have said they would like complete responsibility for welfare, which they would have, of course, with independence or Devo-Max, but not with most of the other proposals put forward for devolution. The findings from the 2012 Scottish Social Attitudes Survey showed that nearly two-thirds (64 per cent) of Scots think that benefit levels should be the responsibility of the Scottish Parliament.[1]

Table 1

Scottish Identifiable Public Expenditure 2011–12*

	£ million	percentage
General public services	1,093	2.0
Public order and safety	2,416	4.4
Economic affairs**	4,961	8.9
Environmental protection	1,056	1.9
Housing and community	1,719	3.1
Health	10,989	19.8
Recreation, culture and religion	1,224	2.2
Education and training	7,702	13.9
Social protection	21,323	38.4
Accounting adjustments	2,999	5.4
Total	55,481	100

*excludes international services, defence and debt interest
**including enterprise and economic development, agriculture, forestry, fishing, employment policies, science and technology and transport

Source: Government Expenditure and Revenue Scotland 2011–2012, *March 2013*

Expenditure per head in Scotland is above the UK average by some 7 per cent and is expected, for demographic reasons, to grow more rapidly, as Professor David Bell has shown in a paper for the Economic and Social Research Council.[2] This is mainly because the proportion of the Scottish population over age 65 is higher and that of the working age population lower than in the UK as a whole. The proportion of elderly is also increasing faster, despite a somewhat lower life expectancy caused by Scotland's poor health record. There is also a higher proportion drawing benefits for illness or disability and expenditure on these tends to increase with age. Thanks to advances in medical care, many more people in all developed countries, including Scotland, are living longer and this involves increasing cost. But the ratio of working population to dependents is the key issue. Although recent figures show that the years of net emigration from Scotland seem to be behind us and the population is growing, it is doing so more slowly than in the UK. This is partly because there has been less immigration to Scotland than to other parts of the UK and also because immigrants tend to have larger families.

In view of its scale, how money is spent on welfare matters a great deal and there is an obvious need to make it as cost-effective as possible, especially at a time when public expenditure throughout the UK is being cut. This applies to Scotland at least as much as to the UK. Several interesting points emerge from the breakdown of the expenditure in Tables 2.1 and 2.2, some of which may be surprising to those who have regarded welfare benefits as something that could and should be cut: the state pension accounts for 45 per cent of the total DWP expenditure and, if other items that are age-related are added, such as Pension Credit, Attendance Allowance and Disability

Table 2.1

*Expenditure by UK Department for Work and Pensions
on Benefits in Scotland 2011–12**

	£million	percentage
Attendance Allowance	482	3.4
Bereavement Benefit/Widow's Benefit	59	0.4
Carer's Allowance	153	1.1
Council Tax Benefit	384	2.8
Disability Living Allowance	1,372	9.8
of which children	109	
of which working age	774	
of which pensioners	488	
Employment and Support Allowance	381	2.7
Housing Benefit	1,728	12.3
Incapacity Benefit	564	4.0
Income Support	670	4.8
of which on Incapacity Benefit	418	
of which lone parents	190	
of which carers	34	
of which others	28	
Industrial Injuries Benefits	93	0.7
Jobseeker's Allowance	461	3.2
Maternity Allowance	24	0.2
Over 75 TV licences	49	0.4
Pension Credit	751	5.3
Severe Disablement Allowance	97	0.7
of which working age	75	
of which pensioners	21	
Statutory Maternity Pay	197	1.4
Winter Fuel Payment	188	1.3
State Pension	6,325	45.2
Total	13,978	100

*excludes tax credits

*Source: Department for Work and Pensions, Expenditure tables, as revised
April 2013*

Living Allowance (DLA) for pensioners, it is more than half. DLA itself, including not only pensioners but also children and those of working age, accounts for almost 10 per cent, and Incapacity Benefit (IB) together with Income Support for those drawing IB, a further 7 per cent. Housing Benefit accounts for 12 per cent. These are the largest items. The cost of unemployment, as shown by expenditure on Jobseeker's Allowance, is only 3.2 per cent – and only 10 per cent if Employment and Support Allowance and Incapacity Benefit are included.

Table 2.2
Scottish Government Expenditure 2011–2012

	£million
Concessionary travel	249
Free prescriptions	57
Free Personal Care	427
Free Nursing Care	23

Source: David Bell's paper 'Social Protection in Scotland' given to the David Hume Institute

Among the items for which the Scottish Government is responsible (see Table 2.2), the cost of free prescriptions is very small when compared with these other items and the cost of concessionary travel at £249 million is more substantial; Free Personal Care and Free Nursing Care at £450 million combined are the most expensive, and are expected to increase considerably as the population ages.

The UK Government's Reforms

The UK Government's reforms to welfare are driven not just by the need to control expenditure; there are also serious faults in the present system. There are a bewildering number of different benefits, as more have been added over the years. This can be confusing to claimants and involves having to fill in numerous claim forms, which some deserving people, especially those with serious disabilities, find difficult. According to the DWP, this can result in some people getting less benefit than they are entitled to and gives scope for fraud. But that is not the only problem – those taking low-paid jobs can lose almost as much in benefit when they start employment as they gain from earnings. This poverty trap has been a problem for many years; it can discourage those on benefit from taking jobs, if the pay they will receive is not significantly more than the benefit they will lose. Everyone has heard anecdotal evidence, whether reliable or not, suggesting that there are some people on benefit who could and should be working. This may well be so, especially if the only job available to an unemployed person involves work that they regard as unpleasant and with a pay that makes them little, if any, better off. I have never been able to understand why some politicians have so strongly argued the case for incentives for the better off, such as bonuses and performance-related pay for businessmen and bankers, while at the same time ignoring the need for incentives for poorer people.

For all these reasons, the need for reform is widely accepted. Given the scale of the task, however, with so many existing types of benefit and tax credits, it is a formidable undertaking and tackling it is bound to throw up unexpected problems. Nevertheless this is what Mr Duncan Smith's Universal Credit is intended to achieve. Reform would be needed just as much in an independent Scotland. But for such a reform to be acceptable, the gain must be clearly seen to outweigh the loss from the inevitable upheaval. The present time is, in many respects, the worst time to be attempting such reform: it would be much easier to achieve if the economy was buoyant, rather than at a time when unemployment is still high, especially among the young, living standards have fallen and the Treasury is determined to achieve savings, even if it causes much resulting hardship.

According to the Government's updated Impact Assessment of December 2012, the replacement of the many existing benefits by Universal Credit, which began to be phased in during 2013, a process that is scheduled for completion by 2017, should actually increase payments to households by £0.3 billion.[3] Most of those gaining, it is claimed, will be among the poorest groups in society. But some 2.8 million households will receive less benefit. So, even if there are more gainers than losers, and the gainers are those most in need, the effect on many people will be very painful. On top of this, the Welfare Benefits Up-rating Act of 2013, which limits the rise in benefits, most tax credits and Universal Credit to only 1 per cent a year, while inflation is running at well above 2 per cent, will result in a much larger number falling into poverty. According to a report for the Scottish Council of Voluntary Organisations, hardship will be increased for many people of working age who are already struggling.[4] In addition to this, there will be a benefit cap of £500 a week for a couple or lone parent and £350 a week for single people. This will apply to all benefits except Disability Living Allowance, War Pensions or Working Tax Credit. There is a real danger that what is an ambitious and necessary reform will be seen just as a savage attempt to save money. Although Universal Credit has only just started to be implemented, the indications so far are not good.

Disability Living Allowance (DLA), which will not be part of Universal Credit, is not means-tested, but many people have simply had their benefit stopped and been made to reapply, no matter how serious or permanent their disability. This is causing great distress, even if benefit is eventually restored, as was shown when a blind man with heart trouble and diabetes, whose benefit had been stopped, gave evidence to the Scottish Parliament. Both the newspapers and television have carried similar stories of cases where the stopping and then reassessment for DLA has caused immense distress. In some of the cases one hears about, the person is so obviously unable to work that one wonders why the benefit was ever stopped. DLA is to be replaced by a Personal Independence Payment (PIP), which, like DLA, is not to be means-tested; however, the budget for it is being cut by 20 per cent and all claimants will have to go through a reassessment process, which will be repeated at intervals. This process itself involves considerable cost to the taxpayer and one may question if it is necessary where a person has a permanent disability.

More than 60 per cent of those on Incapacity Benefit, which was subsumed into Employment Support Allowance (ESA) in 2008, have also had their payments stopped. Although quite a high proportion in these cases also had their benefit restored on appeal, as Martin Sime, chief executive of the Scottish Council for Voluntary Organisations, has said, the effect on many poorer people is likely to push them to despair.

There is also much concern about the proposal for cutting Housing Benefit, if the claimant is assessed as not needing as much accommodation as their current dwelling provides – the so-called 'bedroom tax'. This has attracted the attention of the media and has given rise to a lot of controversy. It is understandable that the state should not pay for more accommodation than is needed; however, unless the assessment is done with care, it can give distressing results. Cases have arisen where a person is told that they have one more bedroom than needed, although a carer uses that bedroom on frequent needed visits. And it makes no sense to cut someone's benefit and tell them they have to move to smaller accommodation if such accommodation is not available in the neighbourhood where carers and others who look after them live.

Inevitably, the cost to the country of welfare benefits goes up when the economy goes into recession. People lose their jobs and swell the ranks of the unemployed, just as tax revenue falls. Many of those who do manage to get work find that only part-time jobs are available or ones that are less well paid than their previous employment. Even if they have a job, some may be drawing benefit in the form of Income Support.

There seems to be a widely held view that public expenditure on welfare is excessive; it is certainly large, but, according to Professor David Bell's analysis, if expenditure on health is included, the UK comes approximately in the middle of the range for European countries – not only the Scandinavian countries but also France, Germany, Italy, the Netherlands and Belgium spend more on social protection as a share of their GDP.[5] The best way of reducing the country's bill for benefits would be to get out of recession and back to full employment, though that would do little to reduce the cost of pensions and welfare benefits for older people, which account for around half of the total cost.

One of the welcome features of the reform, however, is the reduction of the poverty trap by revising the tapering of benefits when a person taking a job starts to earn an income. The present taper can result in a person losing the equivalent of more than 90 per cent of their income. In future, this 90 per cent taper will be reduced to 65 per cent. This is certainly an improvement, but it still means that a person taking a poorly paid job could lose more than half of their income. Reducing the taper is very expensive, as it involves paying out benefit when previously it would have stopped; and it must be one of the reasons the cost of the welfare policy remains so high. But, unfortunately, at a time when the economy is in recession and job opportunities are scarce, it is fanciful to suppose that this will enable many of those who are unemployed to get a job, even if they try their best to find one.

Poverty

The Chancellor unwisely castigated many of those drawing benefit as shirkers, contrasting them with the strivers who found a job and went out to work. The truth is, however, that there are 6.1 million in work drawing benefit because, with low incomes, they are still in poverty, and they out-number the 5.1 million who are not working at all.

Since the late 1990s, according to research done for the Joseph Rowntree Foundation, there had been a welcome reduction in the numbers classified as living in poverty.[6] This was the result of the high level of employment before the financial crisis and of measures, such as tax credits and increases in benefit, introduced by the last government. The Institute for Fiscal Studies calculated that, for lone parents in work, there was an increase in income of 12 per cent, while the proportion of households receiving out-of-work benefits fell by a third.[7] It had been the Labour Government's stated aim to end child poverty by 2020. Obviously the recession has put an end to that, but the prospect now is for the numbers in poverty, both adults and children, to increase.

Over the last 30 years research for the Joseph Rowntree Foundation has shown that inequality in our society has greatly increased, as it has also in the United States and many other countries.[8] The change was greatest in the 1980s, and was particularly marked in London and the south-east of England.[9] In the 1990s, the trend towards greater inequality in incomes continued but at a much slower pace and was largely offset by the tax and benefit system. The better-off, especially but not exclusively in the financial sector, have been able to increase their incomes enormously, while those on the lowest earnings have gained much less and, in some cases, hardly at all. This is a consequence of globalisation, technological change and, in the financial sector, of deregulation. As poorer countries have developed, especially in the Far East, cheap goods have come to Western markets that have kept prices down and forced many manufacturing firms in Europe and North America either to give up production or to reduce costs by restraining the growth of wages so that they can remain competitive. This phenomenon is often described as the 'disappearing middle' – the loss of skilled manual and lower management jobs through computerisation, more advanced capital equipment and competition from abroad.

Professor David Bell and David Eiser of the University of Stirling have shown that inequality in Scotland is much less than in the UK as a whole, since UK figures are affected by those of London and the south-east of England, where inequality is greatest and has grown most. Inequality in Scotland is very similar to that of the rest of England.[10] Scotland comes approximately in the middle of the range for OECD countries, but inequality here is much greater than in any of the Scandinavian countries. It has been increasing there too, however, and at a faster rate.

The growth in inequality runs counter to the kind of

Scotland that many people say they would like to see. With the dominance of SNP and Labour, it is often claimed that Scotland is a more social democratic country than England, where the Conservative Party is still strong. Some commentators writing in the Scottish press have argued for much greater equality of income, citing the example of Scandinavia, or at least for a more caring society with much greater attention paid to the deprived areas in the cities and to those whose prospects of employment and a decent income are poor.[11] This is a type of society that I strongly favour myself, but we do not know what the Scottish electorate as a whole would vote for. Doing more for the less well-off would involve a greater tax burden for the better-off, as in Scandinavia, and the recent Scottish Social Attitudes Survey, despite finding that a majority favoured greater devolution of welfare benefits, did not find that there was an appetite among the general public for this type of redistribution.

The Scottish Government in its white paper argues strongly for a reduction in inequality.[12] It also outlines changes to the social protection system that in my view are desirable, would improve the system itself and would make Scotland a fairer society. It shows that expenditure on social protection forms a lower percentage of total taxation and also of GDP than in the UK as a whole; this is hardly surprising, however, since taxation revenues and GDP from the North Sea are included in these calculations. It goes on to say that 'with independence, we can afford to choose a different path for Scotland, with an approach to social justice that is based on our view of what a healthy and flourishing society should be'. The suggestion is that this could be funded without increasing taxes on the better-off – this is the crucial point, however, and makes the proposals in the white paper more of a manifesto aspiration than a plan. Given the deficit in Scotland's finances, even with North Sea revenues, and particularly in light of the findings in the IFS report referred to in Chapter 1, the statement must be questionable. It would depend on what the country's financial circumstances proved to be after independence and what the then Government's priorities were.

The Scottish Government even now actually possess the powers, with the present amount of devolution, to take action to reduce inequality, if they really wanted to. Such action would not be popular with much of the electorate, but that only illustrates the problem. On the revenue side, they could recalibrate Council Tax, which has never been reformed to reflect increased property values since it was introduced in 1993, despite a tripling in values since that time. If the priority was to help poorer people, it could be structured to take more from wealthy people and less from poorer people. Instead, the government has frozen Council Tax for several years, from which everyone benefits, regardless of income or wealth, and despite the fact that the poorest in society can claim Council Tax Benefit. On the expenditure side, more could be done to help the poorest, if the benefits for which it is responsible, such as free prescriptions, bus passes, free university tuition for Scottish students and care for the elderly, were targeted rather than universal. Universality of benefit is, of course, a prized feature of the welfare state; but with limited resources, and they are likely to remain limited whatever the result of the referendum, a decision has to be made on whether it is more important to maintain that principle or to reduce inequality by doing more for those in genuine poverty. That these changes would not be popular with very many people only illustrates an important truth: that to help the less well-off, something has to be taken from the better-off.

Where Should Responsibility for Welfare Policy Lie?

The discussion so far shows that where responsibility for welfare lies is a major issue in the constitutional debate and is likely to become an increased focus of attention. Not only is it a very important area of policy and a major part of public expenditure, but it might also be expected that the different balance of politics in Scotland should be reflected in policy choices. It is necessary, therefore, to consider what scope for policy choice could be available to a Scottish Government, with both independence and greater devolution.

With independence, the Scottish Government would have complete control of welfare policy and taxation, along with all its other responsibilities. As the white paper says, it would be likely that the then Government would want to do a major review of the taxation and benefit system it inherited. It certainly should do so. Sir James Mirrlees, a distinguished Scottish economist, Nobel Prize winner and member of the First Minister's Council of Economic Advisers, chaired a committee for the Institute for Fiscal Studies that examined the UK tax system. Their report concluded that it was shot through with anomalies and distortions that often conflicted in their purpose and reduced its efficiency.[13] It also concluded that the system provided a disincentive for certain categories of people to seek paid employment, arguing that employment, therefore, might have been substantially greater than it was.

The reforms Mirrlees and his committee put forward are radical and many would be politically difficult, but they also show how the system could be redesigned to produce a more rational system and a fairer society. They may influence future Chancellors of the Exchequer, but certainly any future government of an independent Scotland that set about reviewing the tax and benefit system it inherited should consider them with care.

Independence does not mean that a Scottish Government could act without considering what was happening in the rest of the UK. Scotland is so integrated with the other parts of the UK economy that movement of population across the border would always be very easy. This would mean that if Scotland were more heavily taxed to an extent that was significant, there would be some businesses and people who might move to England; the opposite tendency would be apparent if Scottish taxes were lower than in the remainder of the UK. Differences in welfare provision, if substantial, might also encourage migration. Some people have apparently told those carrying out surveys that they would vote for independence if it made them £500 better off. One should take all this with a pinch of salt. There are some differences in tax rates and welfare provision between Swiss cantons that apparently do not have a huge effect. But the degree of Scotland's integration with the rest of the UK, which would remain even with independence, would certainly have some restraining effect on the scope for independence in policy.

Under various forms of devolution, the issue becomes more complicated. Those who would like to see the whole of welfare expenditure devolved need to consider whether it would acceptable, not only in Scotland but also in the other parts of the UK, for different systems to be applied on each side of the border, while still remaining within one state. Would it be acceptable in Scotland and the rest of the UK, for example, if the state pension and the various benefits for people who are unemployed or have low incomes were at different rates? Despite the apparent support in surveys for much greater devolution of welfare, the response to surveys does not favour that. There would certainly be many who would be strongly against it. Since these are financed at least in part by national insurance contributions, which are at the same rate in Scotland as elsewhere in the UK, people would argue that benefits should also be the same.

Although the main responsibility for welfare rests with the UK Government at present, the Scottish Government is not powerless in this area. Free prescriptions and care for the elderly provide significant welfare benefits. So too does the provision of social housing, action to improve Scotland's areas of acute deprivation and the provision of skill training to help people into jobs. The UK Government's welfare reform will result in responsibility for Council Tax Benefit being devolved. The European Agricultural Policy also provides social benefits that are administered in Scotland, albeit in a way that is not effectively targeted at the poorer members of the farming community.

There are other parts of the welfare programme that seem capable of being devolved. The main test I have applied is whether differences in benefit could be made without fear of significant benefit migration over the border. There could also be difficulty in devolving benefits that are contributory, as different rates in these benefits could be regarded as unfair while national insurance contributions remain the same. This still leaves Housing Benefit, which seems an obvious candidate, as the Scottish Government is responsible for social housing; it would also make sense to devolve Attendance Allowance and Carer's Allowance in view of the Scottish Government's existing responsibilities for health. Other possibilities are TV licences for those over 75, Winter Fuel Payments and Industrial Injuries Benefits, but these three are small. Personal Independence Payment (replacing the Disability Living Allowance) and Severe Disablement Allowance should also be considered; only if extreme would they be likely to encourage benefit migration. These items are all non-contributory and not means-tested. Including Council Tax Benefit, which is already being devolved, they cost £4.5 billion in 2011–12 (see Table 2.1) or almost a third of the present expenditure by the Department for Work and Pensions.

If all of these were devolved and added to the benefits for which the Scottish Government and local authorities already have responsibility, they would make a total of about £10.3 billion, or just under half of the total of £21 billion for social protection in Scotland (see Table 1). The main items excluded would be the state pension and other benefits that are contributory. This would increase the Scottish Government's total expenditure from £38 billion to £43 billion, and therefore reduce the proportion covered by taxes proposed in Chapter 2 for devolution from 57 per cent to 52 per cent. If the benefits I have suggested were devolved, it would greatly add to the Scottish Government's responsibility for welfare and would also provide considerable flexibility. For example, many people do not think that the Winter Fuel Payment should be a universal non-taxable benefit; it could instead be increased for those that are less well off, if it were only paid to people who qualified for other benefits. If these benefits were devolved, it should be remembered that, for demographic reasons, their cost is likely to escalate faster than for the UK as a whole.

Already there is a growing amount of disquiet in England about free prescriptions in Scotland, free care for the elderly and no university tuition fees for Scottish-domiciled students. This is linked to the belief that Scotland gets too generous a share of funding through its block grant. How the grant is settled and whether or not it is too generous has already been discussed in Chapter 1. But differences in welfare provision that are thought to be to the advantage of the Scots would certainly aggravate this concern. If, on the other hand, the English got something that was not available in Scotland, the Scottish population would not be slow to complain.

This leads straight back to how the Scottish Government is funded. The only way in which substantial differences in the benefit system between Scotland and the rest of the UK could be acceptable on both sides of the border would be if they were funded by devolved financial arrangements that people on both sides accepted as fair. It is normal in federal or quasi-federal countries for the central government to at least part-fund the budgets of the component states or regions, even if they have substantial tax powers of their own, but the arrangements need to be acceptable to all parties.[14]

In Scotland's case, the more that can be financed by taxes raised in Scotland, the more readily will differences in provision be accepted. The increased taxation powers available under the Scotland Act 2012 will go some way towards this and, if those taxation powers were increased further, as suggested in Chapter 2, that would again increase flexibility. But, for the remainder, if over the long term it were to prove a durable and defensible arrangement, a smaller block grant from central government would have to be based on a widely accepted system of needs assessment. If Scottish people then wanted a more generous provision of welfare, they would either have to pay more tax, perhaps with a higher rate of Income Tax, or accept that other programmes would need to be cut to provide the resources.

Even with the changes proposed above, which would give substantial responsibility to the Scottish Government and Parliament, and go as far as I think compatible with being in a single state as part of the UK, the responsibility for the remainder, amounting to about half the total expenditure, would remain with the central government. This may seem unsatisfactory to many people who would want to see their government set different priorities from those applied by UK governments, but under any feasible devolution scheme, however much it is adjusted to give more responsibility to Scotland, it seems inevitable that the main direction of taxation and benefit policy has to rest with the UK. Even with independence, although in theory a Scottish Government could set its priorities any way it wished, the real world would impose constraints. There would still be a need to curb public expenditure to balance the budget. And the close economic integration of Scotland with the rest of the UK, which is bound to continue even if it became less over time, would mean that significant differences in tax levels, in state pensions and in welfare could become an issue and result in people moving to where they thought they could get the best treatment.

Pensions and Mortgages

There has been understandable concern about the costs and security of pensions and mortgages, if Scotland were to become an independent state. Would pensions continued to be paid as they are now? Would interest rates on mortgages be higher or lower or remain the same as for the remainder of the United Kingdom? There has been much comment on these questions, some of which has been dismissed, perhaps with justification, as scaremongering; but there are serious issues here that it is the aim of this chapter to explore. They do not arise if Scotland remains within the United Kingdom, regardless of the amount of devolution that may be introduced; but, if there is a prospect of independence, it is quite understandable that they worry people.

Mortgages and Borrowing in an Independent Scotland

The Council for Mortgage Lenders said some time ago that having to comply with separate legal and regulatory systems would increase costs and could therefore lead to more expensive mortgages in Scotland.[1] Owen Kelly, chief executive of Scottish Financial Enterprise, citing similar reasons, has also said that the cost of mortgages would be likely to rise.[2] In one of the economic analysis papers of the UK Government, the Treasury points out that mortgage lenders would be likely to face increased costs in raising funds on the wholesale market; if so, that too would increase the cost of mortgages in Scotland.[3] All of this suggests that the cost of mortgages, and indeed other borrowing, would be higher in an independent Scotland. As the Treasury paper points out, a 1 per cent increase in the mortgage rate for a 75 per cent mortgage on the average house price in Scotland would add some £1,300 to the annual cost.

So far, so bad. On the other hand, Professor Charles Goodhart, a former member of the Bank of England's Monetary Policy Committee and a distinguished expert on the economics of finance has said, 'It can be argued that, provided there is a fully integrated financial services sector, where products can be bought across any boundary between Scotland and a redefined UK, and one common interest rate for the sterling zone, [a difference in mortgage rates] is unlikely to be the case.'[4]

So that is the key. But it now seems most unlikely that a fully integrated financial sector with common interest rates would apply after independence. Even if some form of monetary union continued, it is surely unlikely in the light of the Chancellor's February 2014 speech in Edinburgh that the rest of the UK would agree to have a common sterling debt for Government bonds, because that would mean taxpayers in the rest of the UK and in Scotland standing as guarantors for each other's debt.

Without common sterling debt, Scotland's Government would issue its own bonds, and these would be most unlikely to have lower interest rates than UK bonds, because they would be new on the market without any previous record. Small countries tend, anyway, to have higher interest rates on their debt than larger countries, just because the market for them is more limited. If that proved to be so, the higher interest rates would be reflected across the market and would affect mortgage lenders.

As explained in Chapter 3, if Scotland issued its own currency, even if monetary union continued in some form, that would also give rise to differences in interest rates, depending on how the markets judged the respective security of the Scottish and UK currencies and whether there was any risk of an alteration in the exchange rate.

With separate currencies, even if they are pegged, there is always the possibility that market pressures or differences in economic performance may force exchange rates to be altered. That introduces exchange risk and is the reason why it is very unusual for mortgages or personal loans to be cross-border. To owe money to a company in another country with a different currency can be dangerous. If, for example, the Scottish currency were to depreciate, it could become more expensive to pay a loan back in sterling, if that was the currency in which it was borrowed; on the other hand, if the Scottish currency appreciated in value, the borrower would gain. In the past there were examples of some companies operating in Scotland with loans from foreign banks – for example, in Deutschmarks – that have been made insolvent as a result. It is, therefore, a risk that no individual should take.

The consequence would be that mortgage lenders operating in Scotland would establish branches or subsidiaries operating in the Scottish currency and new loans would be taken out in pounds Scots; but those already holding loans would still have them in sterling, while the assets to which they related, a house or a flat, would have a value in pounds Scots. This would be risky, if at any time the exchange rate between the two currencies were to change. Those holding loans or mortgages in sterling would, therefore, be well advised and might be required by mortgage companies to have them converted into pounds Scots. There might also be a significant number of people with mortgages, or personal and small-business loans, from

English lenders who did not have a presence in Scotland. In such cases the borrowers would be subject to exchange risk; they would then be well advised to pay off their loans and take out fresh ones with companies operating in the Scottish currency.

As a consequence of the financial and economic crisis, the Bank of England lending rate to the other banks is at its lowest since the Bank was founded in 1694. It is bound to rise sooner or later to more normal levels, and that will have an impact on the rates for mortgages, whether provided by banks or building societies. Scotland would be affected in the same way as the rest of the UK if there were monetary union, but if there were no monetary union lending rates would be more likely to differ. Freedom of capital movement would mean that the Scottish central bank would be bound to have regard to rates in the redefined UK in setting its own rates, just as the Bank of England at present takes account of rates set by the European Central Bank and the US Federal Reserve. The question that remains is whether there would also be a premium on Scottish rates over and above the rates elsewhere.

So there are a considerable number of uncertainties for mortgage holders and other borrowers in Scotland, if Scotland becomes independent. Unless there continued to be full integration in financial services, with common interest rates across the border, which seems unlikely, especially in the longer term, it is hard to avoid the conclusion that there would be some increase in the cost of borrowing. And if there were a separate currency, exchange risk would necessitate a reduction in cross-border borrowing. Mortgages, personal loans and loans for business would then have to be taken out in Scottish currency, which would probably only be possible from lenders, whether banks or other mortgage companies, operating in Scotland.

How Secure Would Pensions Be?

Much more has been written about pensions in an independent Scotland than about mortgages. The Institute of Chartered Accountants in Scotland (ICAS) raised questions about Scotland's pensions future in April 2013.[5] The Scottish Government then published a substantial paper in which it sought to allay these concerns in the event of independence.[6] Since the publication of that paper, however, the issues and anxieties have been further elaborated by the National Association of Pension Funds (NAPF).[7]

Pensions are not an easy subject for the average citizen to get to grips with. Indeed for young people, as I remember well from my early days as a university lecturer in Glasgow, it all seems complex and unreal. Eyes tend to glaze over as experts try to explain it. The frequent changes that have been introduced do not make it any easier. But pensions are important, and those who do not pay the subject enough attention early in their careers live to regret it when they come to retire.

The subject divides into three parts. First, there is the existing state pension. Would it continue to be paid in an independent Scotland as at present? Second, how would the many public sector employees in the civil service, the National Health Service and in teaching, hitherto paid directly or indirectly by the UK Government, receive their pensions? And finally, private and company pensions depend on funds built up by the companies and financial institutions; these have to be paid out when the insured person reaches the agreed retirement age. It is over this last group that the most concern has been raised.

The State Pension

The state pension, although notionally contributory through National Insurance, is paid out from general taxation. But it is important to recognise how easily changes with serious consequences can be introduced by governments, whether the UK Government or a potential Scottish Government. As it is unfunded, but paid out of current tax revenue, the pressure on public finances has to be balanced against obligations to pensioners and others who receive public funds. The many changes that have been made over the years illustrate this very clearly.

For example, in the 1980s, payment of the state old-age pension, which had previously been increased annually in line with average earnings, was altered to be up-rated annually using the Consumer Price Index instead, as a cost-saving measure by the then Conservative Government. This saved a substantial amount of public expenditure at the expense of pensioners. The Labour Government in 2002, in response to the concern that this caused, introduced a further change to increase the pension annually by the highest of either the inflation rate measured by the Retail Price Index or by 2.5 per cent.* This was supplemented by means-tested Pension Credit for those whose income on the pension alone was inadequate. Then in 2010 the Coalition Government changed the system again, introducing what is called the triple lock, which will apply until at least 2015.[8] This increases the state pension annually by whichever is the greater: the increase in average earnings, inflation measured by the Consumer Price Index or 2.5 per cent a year.

Despite this latest change, the state pension will not recover the ground lost since the 1980s and is now one of the lowest state pensions in Europe.[9] In contrast to many other European countries, the tradition in the UK has been to rely

* The RPI includes the cost of mortgage interest payments and Council Tax, which are not included in the CPI, while some other items are. The result is that inflation as measured by the two indices differs from month to month, with sometimes one and sometimes the other showing the greater increase.

heavily on the private sector either as company occupational schemes or private pensions invested by individuals with life assurance companies. According to the Scottish Government's white paper, however, only about half the Scottish population are covered by occupational or private pensions. To the remainder, the state pension, though not generous, is crucially important.[10]

The UK Government, as well as introducing the triple lock for up-rating the present state pension, has now announced a new single-tier state pension from April 2017. This is to replace the existing complex system, which included the Second State Pension, contracting out, Pension Credit and various out-of-date additions.[11] Up-rating of this new system will be decided from year to year, but in January 2014 the Prime Minister, following a similar commitment made by the Scottish Government, announced that if his party formed the government after the forthcoming general election, the triple lock would continue for the life of the next Parliament. In 2013, the value of the new pension is expected to start at a flat rate of £144 a week, or £7,488 a year (compared with £110.15, or £5,728 a year, at present for the basic state pension alone). This is estimated to be above the level at which means-tested Pension Credit becomes available to those whose income is inadequate and it will, therefore, be discontinued.

The full pension will be paid to those who have made national insurance contributions for 35 years. For those who do not have the full 35 years of contributions, there will be a pro-rata reduction, subject to a minimum qualifying period. However, in line with forecasts for improved life expectancy and to make the cost of the pension sustainable, the qualifying age will rise from 65 to 66 years by October 2020, and to 67 between 2026 and 2028. In his Autumn Statement 2013, the Chancellor said he expected the qualifying pension age to go on rising to 68 in the late 2030s, 69 sometime in the 2040s and with the prospect that it could rise to 70 after 2050. A review of the state pension age will be carried out every five years to ensure that the costs are shared fairly between the generations. Although life expectancy is expected to continue to rise, the problem is that many older people suffer from chronic health problems that make them unfit or unable to work as they once did.

The Scottish Government's proposals, set out in a paper on pensions in September 2013 and in the white paper, build on the UK Government's scheme.[12] By 2016, the UK pension is expected to have risen to £158.90 a week, or £8,262.80 a year, and the Scottish Government is proposing £160 a week, or £8,320. It is also proposed that the triple lock would continue for the life of the first Parliament after independence. According to the white paper, the element of Pension Credit, which guarantees a minimum income, would be included in the triple lock, and Savings Credit, which provides an extra payment for those who have saved something towards their retirement, would be retained. The Scottish Government accepts the UK Government's increase in the state pension age to 66 in 2020 but proposes that the further increase to 67 should be subject to review by an independent commission to take account of Scotland's lower life expectancy.

There is a strong flavour of political manifesto about these proposals. Although the differences are not very great, there is an undisguised attempt at each point to offer something better than the UK Government. Like political manifestos generally, however, it will in the event depend on what can be afforded. Past experience has shown that governments do not hesitate to make changes, if compelled to do so by economic circumstances, and the work of the Institute for Fiscal Studies described in Chapter 1 does not suggest that it will be easy to avoid an increasing fiscal deficit in future years, as revenues from the North Sea decline and Scotland's demographic structure imposes additional burdens.

Public Sector Pensions

Like the state pension, most public sector pensions are unfunded; only the Local Government Pension Scheme is operated as a funded scheme. For many of those that are unfunded, employees and employers pay contributions, but there is no dedicated fund into which these are paid and then invested. In total, these contributions may either exceed or fall short of the amounts to be paid out in a particular year. Where this is so, in the case of the NHS and teachers schemes the balance is either paid over to or made up from UK Government tax revenues; and in the case of police and firefighters schemes, by the Scottish Government.

The operation of NHS and teachers pension schemes is handled by the Scottish Public Pensions Agency for which financial management responsibility rests with the UK Treasury. The Local Government Pension Scheme is managed by 11 local authorities, while the schemes for police and firefighters are also locally managed; but all of these schemes must comply with UK legislation – only in the case of a small number of public bodies, certain judicial office-holders working for devolved bodies, and for its own members does the Scottish Parliament have policy and legislative control. Pensions for the civil service in Scotland and for the armed services are paid by the UK Government and are entirely under the control of the UK Parliament.

With independence, responsibility for paying all of these pensions would transfer to Scotland. The Scottish Government has given an assurance that those already retired, as well as those who will retire in future, will have their pensions fully protected. Where a person who has worked in the public sector in Scotland, a civil servant for example, retires to live in England, payment of his or her pension would also be made by the Scottish Government. But there are, nevertheless, important matters to be negotiated. There could be many cases where a retired person worked for part of his or her life in Scotland but the rest in other parts of the UK; responsibility for payment in such cases would be more complicated.

A future government of an independent Scotland would be free to set retirement ages for public sector employees as it saw fit and these might increasingly diverge from ages set in the rest of the UK. In line with the recommendations of the Hutton Commission, there is no proposal to change the unfunded public sector pensions to any sort of funded scheme.[13] Since there is no dedicated fund, there is no question to moving to a Defined Contribution (DC) system, but steps have already been taken to move away from Defined Benefit (DB) based on final salary; the DB system was to the advantage of those ending their careers in senior positions with high salaries, since it gave them a pension set as a percentage of final salary. This is being replaced by a pension based on Career Average Revalued Earnings (CARE). The Scottish Government has said this would take effect for those retiring from 2015.

The Local Government Pension Scheme, which is a funded scheme, has assets that broadly match its liabilities, with a funding level of approximately 95 per cent in 2011. Other smaller funded schemes for devolved bodies are similarly supported by dedicated funds.

Unfunded pension liabilities for the public sector in Scotland, however, are extremely large. Excluding non-departmental public bodies, some of which are unfunded, they are estimated by the Institute of Chartered Accountants in

Scotland to total at least £60.2 billion. This is without the substantial liabilities that would be transferred to Scotland for the civil service and armed forces schemes in the event of independence. Defining the Scottish Government's responsibility for the civil service in Scotland would be relatively straightforward, but it is much less clear how the armed services might be divided and in consequence how much of the responsibility and share of cost would have to be taken over. Like these schemes in the rest of the UK, unfunded schemes currently pay out more in pensions than they receive in contributions and the gap is thought likely to grow. With independence, it would be for the Scottish Government to decide how this should be handled: for example, whether an increasing amount of the cost should be funded by tax revenue or by increased contributions. Scotland might decide to tackle this differently from the redefined UK, but the implications could be substantial.

Private Sector Pensions

Although occupational and private pensions form a very large part of the incomes of retired people in the UK who receive them, it has not been a happy experience for many pensioners. Only about half of the Scottish population have such pensions, so that this is one of the main causes of income inequality referred to in the last chapter. Furthermore, participation in such schemes has declined rather than increased. Private sector pension scheme membership in the UK is now less than half what it was in 1967. Proportionately, membership in Scotland seems to be higher than in the rest of the UK, but it has still fallen.[14] Part of the reason for this may be the sharp reduction in the percentage of employees in manufacturing industry, where many would have been automatically enrolled, but it may also be due to the disappointing performance, indeed failure, of some of the schemes, which has discouraged people from joining them.

One might have expected private and company pension schemes that are funded to be less dependent on action by government. But this is not the case. Governments of both major parties have intervened in ways that damaged the value of pensions. The Conservative Government's Financial Services Act of 1986 ended the requirement for employees to be in occupational schemes. The Act also removed tax exemption on pension fund surpluses. Companies with funds in surplus over what was needed to match their liabilities had been able to deduct the full amount as a cost before profit was assessed for Corporation Tax. Ending this tax exemption in good times only discouraged companies from building up such surpluses and meant that funds failed to match liabilities when the market suffered a fall. Then, in 1997, the Labour Government ended Advance Corporation Tax Relief for pension funds. This change, for which Gordon Brown, the Chancellor of the Exchequer at the time, has been blamed, cost pension funds an estimated £5 billion a year, reducing dividend income by about 20 per cent.[15] Most of the schemes remained profitable, however, until the stock market crashed in 2001. At that point, when the market for equity shares was at its most depressed, the regulator required pension companies to rebalance their portfolios, apparently to safeguard the interest of pensioners. But selling large amounts of equity stock, when the market was already at its lowest for many years, only depressed equity prices further and buying fixed interest stock with these depleted funds pushed up the price of gilts and other bonds. The resulting large loss in value was never recouped.

It is, therefore, not surprising that many occupational and private pension funds have been in difficulty. The bankruptcy of the Equitable Life Assurance Society graphically illustrated the problem. In the early 1960s, I had to choose into which life assurance company I should invest my pension under the then university scheme. The information I was given showed that Equitable Life gave the best return. At its peak it had 1.5 million policy holders and £26 billion under management. But in 2000 it closed to new business because it had failed to make sufficient allowance for adverse market changes. Attempts to find a buyer failed and a great many policy holders lost a lot of their money. Mercifully, later in my career, I had transferred what I had invested into another pension scheme. But many people did not, or were unable to do so, and were left with pension income amounting to only a fraction of what they had expected.

In 2008, the Parliamentary and Health Service Ombudsman found the Government guilty of ten counts of maladministration and called for a compensation scheme. It was estimated that 30,000 policy holders had died without compensation. A government compensation scheme is now in place, but payments are still (as at 2013) being made at the rate of £1 million a day and the Treasury has had to extend the life of the scheme to 2015 because it has still been unable to trace 400,000 policy holders. This is an extreme case, but many pension companies have assets that are still insufficient to fund their liabilities. In time it is expected that companies will be able to resolve this by building up their assets and repairing their balance sheets.

A consequence is that many company schemes that gave the pensioner a fixed percentage of final salary on retirement, Defined Benefit (DB), have been changed to a pension based on contribution – Defined Contribution (DC). This means that what a pensioner will receive will depend on the market: how much he or she has paid into the scheme, how the funds from his or her accumulated contributions have been invested, what they are worth at the time of retirement and what the rate on annuities happens to be at that time. This introduces a huge element of uncertainty. If a person retires when the market is high, he or she could do as well or even better than with a DB pension; but if retirement co-incides with a slump in the market, the annuity that could be bought with the maturing fund could result in a disap-pointing pension. Before the financial crisis, almost all com-panies offering occupational pensions did so on a DB basis; now, almost all offer their employees only a DC pension.

Pension investment as a form of saving has always been en-couraged with substantial tax relief. The cost of both occupa-tional and private pensions can be paid from pre-tax income, resulting in a substantial saving of both standard and higher rates of tax. Recently, as a result of the very large earnings some people have been receiving, a ceiling of £50,000 has been imposed on the amount that can be invested in a pen-sion in any one year. Anything above this is subject to tax.

In view of what has happened, it is not surprising that confidence in the industry has been badly shaken and that over the UK as a whole 13.2 million people are estimated to be under-saving for their retirement. Both private pen-sions and occupational pensions have been affected. A fur-ther problem has been that annuity rates have been very low in the last few years, with the result that money from a pension fund, when invested in an annuity, has resulted in a disappointing pension. This is partly an unavoidable consequence of the Bank of England's unprecedentedly low lending rate to help the recovery of the economy and the Bank's policy of buying gilts as part of its quantitative eas-ing programme. This, combined with private investors turn-ing to gilts and fixed rate bonds for security in a depressed stock market, has pushed up prices and kept interest rates exceptionally low on government stock in which a large part of pension funds is invested. For many of those who had invested in pensions, the income achievable has been disappointing. In some cases, people investing have felt misled when their pensions have fallen well below what they had been led to expect by a pension company; there have been accusations of mis-selling and some claims for compensation have been upheld.

The Coalition Government, as part of its reform of pensions, has now introduced automatic enrolment in an attempt to address the problem of under-saving. This reverses the provision in the 1986 Act, which freed employers from this obligation. Employers now have a duty to enrol all employees who are at least 22 years old in a DC workplace pension, unless the employee specifically asks to be exempted; and it is expected that many more employees across Scotland will now be enrolled, some for the first time. However, this process will take time. To help employers fulfil their duty to enrol their employees, the new National Employment Savings Trust (NEST) provides a scheme focused on those with low or moderate earnings. The scheme is also open to those who are self-employed.

The Scottish Government have said that, in the event of a vote for independence, it plans no changes to tax relief on occupational or private pensions; it would continue automatic enrolment; and it would work with the UK Government to ensure that both employers and employees continued to have access to NEST. It also envisages that a Scottish equivalent to this scheme would in due course be set up.

If Scotland becomes independent, however, there could be implications for pension companies both in Scotland and elsewhere in the UK. If Scotland remains in monetary union with the rest of the UK, the Scottish Government clearly hopes that some at least of the UK institutions would continue to operate in Scotland with minimal change. The body of law governing pensions in Scotland would continue to apply until such time as a Scottish government decided to make amendments. This would also apply to the regulatory framework, although after independence the Scottish Government has said it would set up a Scottish Pensions Regulator.[16] It is proposed that this body would work closely with the UK regulator and the UK Financial Conduct Authority.

The Pensions Act of 2004 established the Pension Protection Fund (PPF) in response to public concern when employers sponsoring Defined Benefit (DB) pension schemes became insolvent. The Fund provides compensation to scheme members affected by insolvencies and is financed by a levy on participating schemes. Only DB schemes and the DB part of hybrid schemes based in the UK are eligible. Assessment is triggered by the insolvency of a scheme and a valuation is then conducted of its assets and liabilities to see whether the scheme could afford to purchase annuities at or above the level of compensation. Only if it cannot does the PPF provide compensation, in which case it takes over the scheme's assets. The Scottish Government has said that it would expect an independent Scotland to play its full part in these arrangements, but this would need to be part of a post-independence negotiation with the UK Government. It would be open to a future Scottish Government to set up a Scottish equivalent to PPF.

It will be apparent that the future of pensions in an independent Scotland hinges to a great extent on whether it proves possible for Scotland to remain in some form of monetary union with the rest of the UK. If this does not prove possible, either because the remainder of the UK refuses to agree or because at some stage the Scottish Government considers that the conditions are too restrictive, it would be much less likely that Scotland could continue to participate in UK institutions. Separate institutions, or at least Scottish branches of institutions based elsewhere in the UK, would then have to be established. A separate currency, even if pegged to sterling, would also introduce considerable uncertainty for pension holders. If the currency peg were at some stage removed, or the exchange rate altered, in what currency would pensioners be paid and what might their pensions then be worth? If the pension was taken out with a Scottish pension provider, presumably the pensioner would be paid as before, but in the new Scottish currency. If, on the other hand, it was an English scheme, exchange risk becomes involved. The pension, unless arrangements had been made otherwise, would be paid in sterling and that might be worth either less or more in the Scottish currency, depending on the movement of exchange rates. This is why pension schemes generally do not cross national boundaries. Indeed, within the EU, the UK was only the home state for 28 such schemes and half of those were with the Irish Republic.[17]

This was the problem highlighted by the Institute of Chartered Accountants for Scotland (ICAS). The EU's IORP Directive makes it possible for institutions to provide pensions across national borders and was intended to be a step towards providing pensions on a European scale, but the Directive requires schemes to be fully funded, with assets at least matching their liabilities, if they accept contributions from employers in another member state. If Scotland becomes a separate state from the rest of the UK, but within the EU, this Directive would apply and those UK schemes that are not at present fully funded would have a problem. ICAS suggested that schemes might either seek an exemption or a grace period during which they had to comply. They might have to reconstruct themselves into separate Scottish and 'rest of UK' schemes, although this would not solve the funding problem. The danger is, of course, that if they had to comply immediately, a number of the schemes could be forced into insolvency.

Provided there is goodwill and a readiness to compromise, it should be possible to negotiate a transition period during which the schemes could become fully funded. After all, no one would think it right for such schemes to be underfunded indefinitely. Nor presumably would the rest of the EU think it right for this to become a roadblock, when the purpose of the Directive was not to hinder but to promote the development of an integrated internal market in financial services. But getting all the schemes onto a fully funded basis could be a lengthy process; and it offers yet another problem for any EU member state to exploit, if it was minded to try to stop a country seceding from a member state from becoming a member in its own right.

Conclusion

There are many issues relating both to mortgages and pensions that have to be considered if Scotland becomes independent. Whether some form of monetary union with the rest of the UK continues is a key issue. Without full integration, mortgage rates would be likely to be higher in an independent Scotland than for the rest of the UK. A separate currency would necessitate mortgage borrowing to be reconstructed to avoid the exchange risk that cross-border borrowing would imply. People would then arrange mortgages for their houses or flats either from purely Scottish institutions or with the branches or subsidiaries of the UK institutions that were able to lend in the Scottish currency. That could imply different and possibly higher interest rates for the reasons explained.

For pensions, some of the same issues apply and there is the additional complication of the EU's IORP Directive, which requires cross-border schemes to be fully funded, although this, one would hope, could be dealt with by agreeing a transition period in negotiation. The Scottish Government has given very clear assurances that people with state pensions would not be any worse off in an independent Scotland and has sought to improve on the pensions that the UK Government is set to provide. But no one expects financial resources to be anything other than restricted for years to come, either in Scotland or the UK.

Governments have in the past made changes that have left state pensioners worse off and damaged the funds on which private pensioners depend. One hopes that not only future UK governments but also potential Scottish governments have learnt not to change the rules at the expense of pensions again.

There can be no guarantee against damaging changes in future, however, either in Scotland or the UK, because the problem of affording pensions for a growing proportion of elderly people in the population is one of the pressing issues of our time.

10

Conclusion

As the date of the referendum on Scottish independence draws near, there are those who say they have not had enough information to make an informed decision. This should not be a problem now. The Scottish Government's massive white paper and the detailed papers in the Scotland Analysis series published by the UK Government provide a wealth of information. None of these, however valuable, is entirely impartial. This is not a book beholden to either the independence or the 'Better Together' campaigns; its purpose has been to try to set out the issues for both independence and a greater degree of devolution so that people can better understand what would be involved before voting.

Those supporting Scottish independence sometimes point out that few, if any, of the countries that have seceded from a larger state regret that decision. Certainly, the Irish Republic would not want to come back into the United Kingdom, nor Iceland to Denmark or Norway to Sweden; nor probably would the countries that have left the Soviet Union want to go into union again with Russia. But, in the case of Scotland, there has been no history of exploitation or bad government, such as fuelled the drive for independence in Ireland. Scotland is among the wealthier countries in Europe, with a GDP per head (excluding the North Sea) approximately equal to that of the UK and an unemployment rate very similar. Immigration has replaced net emigration and, on most measures, Scotland's economy is in a better relative position compared with the UK as a whole than 30 years ago. Scotland could perfectly well be independent, if that is what the people choose. Its economy is certainly much stronger than Ireland's was in 1922. I accept also that there are circumstances that can enable a small country to do better economically, if it is independent than if it is part of a larger state, and I set this out in Chapter 3.

But that does not mean that the process of separation would be easy or painless. It would be a major upheaval, with uncertain consequences. After more than 300 years of union Scotland's economy has become very integrated with the rest of the UK. This applies especially to the capital and labour markets. We also share many of the same institutions. Breaking this up would certainly involve costs in disengagement, with the potential for damage to some important industries, especially perhaps the financial sector. There are many uncertainties – the currency, membership of the EU, energy policy and pensions, for example – that need to be clarified. I have argued in the book that some of these – for example, membership of the EU – might not be as much of a problem as it is sometimes represented. But the truth is that no one can say for certain until negotiations actually take place.

The Implications of Independence

Like the rest of the UK, Scotland has been badly hit by the recession in the last five years. This is because, like several other countries in Europe, notably Ireland and Spain, the previous boom was fuelled in the UK by ever-expanding private debt, much of it associated with housing. Rising personal debt meant that people were living beyond their means. When this came spectacularly to an end, the consequences and necessary adjustment were, and will remain for some years yet, extremely difficult and painful. At the time of writing, the UK budget deficit is still too high, public debt is high and still rising, and the Chancellor has just announced that the austerity he has imposed to correct this will go on and even be tightened further at least until 2018. If the Scottish people decide in the 2014 referendum that they want their country to become an independent state again, these difficult circumstances would apply to Scotland too and do not make it the easiest time to choose.

The first major problem would be with the Scottish Government's own finances. The SNP Government argues that Scotland's deficit is smaller proportionately than that of the UK, but that depends on some key assumptions, set out in Chapter 1: first, that Scotland would get, as its geographical share, some 90 per cent of the North Sea oil revenues; and second, that the UK national debt would be divided on a population basis, rather than its share of UK GDP, including GDP from the North Sea. The SNP Government has said it would accept a population share but have also argued that the share should be less than this because oil revenues since 1980 mean that Scotland has contributed more than its share to public finances over these years.

All of this would be subject to negotiation, the outcome of which must remain uncertain until negotiations for independence actually take place. There is, at present, no formal division of the North Sea between England and Scotland, and negotiations between the UK and other countries over their share of the Continental shelf have not always been straightforward. And, after all that is settled, it would be up to the markets to decide what rate of interest had to be paid on Scotland's share of the debt and on any new borrowing. Since those who own UK debt would probably not be happy with a share of it simply being transferred, the mechanism would probably either involve the Scottish Government agreeing to pay interest on its share of the debt to the UK Government until all of it was paid off, or having to float its own debt for the amount to be transferred and then paying the proceeds to the UK Government so that the appropriate share of the UK debt could be redeemed. If Scottish debt interest rates were higher than on UK debt, the latter course would be likely to be the most costly.

For many years, Scotland has had a level of public expenditure per head that has been 10 per cent or more above that of the UK. With taxation revenue per head, excluding the North Sea, about equal to that of the UK, this leaves a gap that revenue from the North Sea would be needed to fill, unless expenditure was cut sharply or other taxes raised. Even with this, there is, at present, an unsustainable deficit, as there is also for the UK, which is why the UK Government has had its programme of austerity. Unfortunately, the output of both oil and gas from the North Sea is now well past its peak, although the life of both has been prolonged as a result of new discoveries and advances in technology. There is a substantial difference between the Office for Budget Responsibility's estimates of future oil and gas revenues and those of the Scottish Government, as explained in Chapter 7. The latter are higher, with an increase for a few years as a result of the recent high levels of investment. But both expect a gradual decline thereafter.

The Institute for Fiscal Studies, taking account of this decline in oil and gas revenues and also of Scotland's more rapidly ageing population, found that on present policies there would be a continued deterioration in the Scottish deficit so that it became larger in future while that of the UK would stabilise by 2016–17. Oil and gas revenues, however, are extremely hard to predict, as they depend not only on output but also on prices. In addition to the normal uncertainties, the potential impact of 'fracking' (the process of hydraulic fracturing for oil and gas that has had a big impact on energy prices in America) makes forecasting future prices exceptionally difficult. As a result of both the price and output variations, revenues have been very volatile, even in the last four years – they have varied between £12.9 billion in 2008–09 for the UK, down to £6.5 billion in 2009–10, up again to £11.3 billion in 2011–12 and down to £6.5 billion in 2012–13. This volatility could make a Scottish budget difficult to manage.

Alex Salmond has said that, as soon as circumstances allow, an independent Scottish Government would put part of the oil revenues into a special fund, as Norway has done. I welcome that. It was a great economic opportunity missed that successive UK Governments have not done this over the last 30 years. It would have transformed the UK's financial position. But, in the immediate future, Scotland would be unable to afford it. Even with the oil and gas revenues, there would be a budget deficit, as was shown in Chapter 1. If it were to do this, a Scottish government would either have to raise other taxes or bring public expenditure down to the same level as the UK average.

A large proportion of the North Sea hydrocarbon resources are in waters off the Northern Isles. Shetland and Orkney both had the foresight to set up oil funds from which they have got considerable benefit. They are concerned now about a tendency towards centralisation of Holyrood governments and issues have been raised by their MSPs about their constitutional status within Scotland. The Scottish Government would be well advised to discuss this with them.

Despite many assertions that Scottish control of economic levers would result in higher economic growth to pay for this, no one has really explained how that is to be achieved. The Scottish Government's stated policy is to reduce Corporation Tax to 3 per cent below the UK level to encourage investment, but that is likely to be resisted by the rest of the UK because of its potential distorting effect, if Scotland wants to remain in the sterling monetary union. Various other measures are suggested in the white paper, such as targeted depreciation allowances, supporting innovation, support for small- and medium-sized businesses, and strengthening the role of the Scottish Investment Bank. Much of this could be done even with devolution, as was shown in Chapter 2. Already one of the main areas of public expenditure where more is spent in Scotland per head than in the UK is economic affairs. More recently the First Minister has said that independence would enable more to be spent on childcare, thereby enlarging the labour force and raising the potential for economic growth, but while that could be important in the longer term, it would add to costs immediately and depend on jobs being available so that tax revenue increased.

The choice of currency would be of crucial importance. The Scottish Government has made it clear that it would want to retain sterling and for the Bank of England to remain lender of last resort. But, in the light of the Chancellor's Edinburgh speech, this now seems very unlikely to be acceptable, even if there was in the speech an element of trying to reinforce the NO campaign in the referendum. With a looser from of monetary union and a Scottish central bank issuing a Scottish currency, so long as the Scottish currency was pegged to sterling, there would still be no scope for significant differences in monetary policy from the rest of the UK; and the Bank of England would set its policy to meet the needs of the UK without Scotland.

Such a union would also impose constraints on fiscal policy in order to keep the exchange rate pegged. These constraints would not be so tight as with a full formal monetary union, but the market would soon react adversely if it was thought that policies in Scotland were putting the pegged exchange rate at risk. Even with a fiscally conservative policy, there would be a risk that it might not last, as the break-up of the Czech and Slovak monetary union after only six weeks (see Chapter 3) clearly illustrated. There could be a dangerous period of uncertainty after a YES vote in the referendum, while negotiations were in progress. Everything would have to be done to avoid this, since it could result in bank deposits moving out of Scotland to the security of sterling in other parts of the UK. This is exactly what happened in Slovakia, when massive funds moved to the Czech Republic, thereby causing the collapse of the monetary union.

After independence, I would expect Scotland and the rest of the UK to diverge gradually in the policies they followed. Whether the SNP or Labour were dominant in Scotland, the balance in Scottish politics would be likely to be Social Democratic, whereas the UK, especially without Scottish members in Parliament, would be more likely to be Conservative. Scotland may wish to become a bit more like Scandinavia, with its comprehensive welfare system and relatively egalitarian society, whereas the rest of the UK, and England especially, might put more emphasis on a low tax, low public expenditure free market economy, like the United States. If that happened, it could put severe strain on a monetary union. For these reasons, while I think it would be sensible for Scotland to have some form of monetary union with the rest of the UK, it might prove difficult in the long run to maintain it.

In view of the Chancellor's intervention and that of the spokesmen for the other two parties at Westminster, it seems virtually certain that Scotland would have to have its own currency, and monetary union would then involve that being pegged to sterling, just as the Danish krone is presently pegged to the euro. That would be the much missed

Plan B. It has advantages because in a really serious crisis, to avoid the kind of stresses that we have seen in the eurozone, the exchange rate could be adjusted. Any risk of exchange rate adjustment, however, would be reflected in the interest rates the market would demand on Scottish Government bonds and there would also be important implications for financial companies that operate across the border.

The financial sector in Scotland is one of its most important industries and has grown greatly over the last 20 years to the point where it now employs some 100,000 people. The government would, therefore, have to think carefully about how it should be handled in the event of independence. The collapse of Scotland's two largest banks was a disaster keenly felt by many Scots, who regarded them as part of Scotland's distinctive identity. To many, they had been a source of some pride. But excessive growth and mergers had transformed them and put them at risk. If Scotland had been independent at the time of the 2008 crisis, I believe that their problems would have overwhelmed the country's finances, just as the insolvency of the Irish banks did in Ireland.

It is important to learn from that experience so that, if Scotland does become independent, policies are in place to ensure that it could never be repeated. This means not only tight regulation and not having institutions that are too big to fail but also ensuring that Scottish-based banks and other financial institutions trading outside Scotland do so through subsidiaries, rather than branches, so that they are subject to the regulations and the deposit insurance scheme of the country where they operate. Probably the two large banks would both decide to operate from headquarters in London, with Bank of Scotland and Royal Bank as subsidiary companies separately regulated in Scotland. This would be the least risky arrangement for Scotland, but it would imply losing the RBS headquarters at Gogar, outside Edinburgh.

Keeping some sort of monetary union would probably help other financial companies to remain in Scotland, because without it, some of those whose client base was not in Scotland, such as Standard Life, might wonder if they would be better to base their activities south of the border. This also applies to the investment trusts and fund managers, all of which contribute greatly to the economy. Only the companies can say what they would do, but their needs and likely actions must be clarified so that the Scottish Government is aware of the issues that are at stake and can attempt to take them into account in formulating policy.

It is clear that there would need to be negotiations for Scotland to become a full member of the European Union in its own right. The key to a successful outcome would be the goodwill of all the present 28 member states. If there were such goodwill, it should be possible, as Sir David Edward has argued, for this to be done by treaty amendment rather than by the full process of joining the queue of candidate members and negotiating an accession treaty. It would also be reasonable to expect the other member states to agree conditions that would include opt-outs from the Schengen Agreement and the euro. But any one state could exercise a veto and, even if it did not go so far as that, it could insist on no opt-outs or on conditions that caused difficulties. It would be unreasonable, but the risk is that a country such as Spain, even if it did not go so far as to use its veto, might resist agreement to any concessions because of worry about the precedent for a secession movement in its own territory.

I see no prospect of Scotland being able to retain a share of the UK rebate. Circumstances have changed since the UK rebate was originally negotiated and most countries would like to see it ended. Scotland would get substantial payments both from the Common Agricultural Policy and the Structural Funds and, although it would be making a net contribution to the EU budget, it would probably be no higher per head than that of several other countries.

The Scottish referendum will take place before the UK referendum on continued membership of the EU that Prime Minister David Cameron has promised, if his party gain an outright majority after the next election. This commitment appears to be partly a consequence of a growing English nationalism, the most obvious manifestation of which is the rise in support for the United Kingdom Independence Party (UKIP); but there is also irritation with rules and directives, many of which are associated with the single market. Encouraged by a strongly euro-sceptic press, opinion, especially in the south of England and in parts of the Conservative Party, is now actively hostile to the EU. Indeed, as this book goes to press there is news that a large number of Conservative backbenchers are pressing for legislation to ensure the EU referendum takes place and many of them also support a proposal that the UK Parliament should have power to veto EU legislation. As the Foreign Secretary has pointed out, the EU would be unworkable if all countries had this power.

All this creates a difficulty for Scotland. If Scotland becomes independent and negotiates to stay in the EU but the rest of the UK then votes to leave, that could mean border posts at Gretna, Carter Bar and Berwick. The present expectation of those who wish to leave the EU, however, is that they could maintain a free-trading relationship and be within the single market, perhaps as a member of the European Economic Area (EEA). That may not be as straightforward as they assume. The other possibility is that, if Scotland votes to stay in the UK but then in the UK referendum also votes for continued EU membership while England votes to leave, it could create a difficult political situation and be a source of tension between the two governments. This might eventually lead to a second Scottish referendum, if the consequence of being no longer in the EU was widely seen as damaging to Scotland.

Scottish membership of the EU is very important because so many inward investing companies, which have contributed much to the economy, have only chosen Scotland because it is a good base from which to serve the European market. If Scotland were outside the EU, it would be more difficult to attract inward investment and some international companies already here might consider leaving. This would depend on what agreement was reached on access to the single market. Even if Britain were in the EEA, however, companies might prefer to locate in Ireland, Scotland's main competitor for such investment, simply because it was a full EU member.

Trade negotiations with countries outside the EU are conducted by the European Commission on behalf of all the member states. This is a major benefit. In a world that is becoming increasingly dominated by large powers, such as Brazil, Russia, India and China (known as 'the BRIC countries'), as well as the United States, small European countries acting on their own would have very little clout in such negotiations. So the need for inward investment, unrestricted access to the EU single market and influence in trade negotiations all make membership of the EU of great importance to Scotland. If, therefore, it seemed increasingly likely that the UK would leave the EU, a logical consequence could be an increase in support for independence.

Scotland has energy resources that many European countries might envy, even excluding North Sea oil. Output of renewable energy is increasing and will supply a growing proportion of our electricity, though at the same time the visual impact of more and more wind turbines on the landscape means it is encountering ever-stronger opposition. Apart from this, although land-based wind power may be economic by the second half of this decade, according to forecasts, it is still not cheap and its output is highly variable; offshore wind power has better availability and will perhaps be regarded as less visually intrusive, but it will have to be subsidised for many years, as will wave or tidal power, which are still only in the very early stages of development.

More than a quarter of the electricity generated in Scotland is exported via interconnectors to England and Northern Ireland, and the subsidy for renewable energy, regardless of where it comes from, is paid by consumers throughout Britain. That is a cost that Scottish consumers would find excessive if they alone had to bear it and an independent Scotland probably could not afford. Whether the rest of the UK would be prepared to continue paying for it would depend on how seriously the UK Government regarded its commitments to reducing carbon emissions and also on whether it was possible to get cheaper supplies from elsewhere. This might be from either more investment in other parts of the UK, through the interconnector with Continental Europe or from Ireland, which has plans for a major expansion in renewable energy that it hopes to export.

Scotland's energy policy at present is based on a target, announced by the First Minister, that requires the equivalent of all its electricity to come from renewable sources by 2020. It is very doubtful if this will be achievable because of increased hostility from the public to wind turbines and the intermittent nature of their availability. Chapter 6 showed that a lot can be done to tackle this, both through pump storage hydropower and by connecting to a larger area, but the problem remains. Nuclear power does not emit carbon, but the Scottish Government has so far been unwilling to contemplate renewal of its two nuclear stations, despite their excellent performance and safety record. They do not come to the end of their lives for at least another ten years, but replacement would be very expensive and would have to be planned many years in advance.

So far the Scottish Government has given no support to 'fracking' for gas or oil, which is now supported in England by the UK Government. Scotland has geology that indicates that this could be a major resource – and while gas from fracking would emit carbon, it would be very much less than from coal. It makes little sense to be in favour of exploiting offshore oil and gas to the maximum extent possible but at the same time not exploiting the resource on land. If the example of the United States is anything to go by, it could give Scotland a cheap source of energy that could greatly benefit consumers and improve the competitive position of industry in Scotland. It could also replace coal in the generation of electricity and, because of its flexibility for electricity generation, it fits well with renewable power sources, complementing their availability.

Independence would present some serious problems for mortgages and pensions. Markets are likely to require higher interest rates on Scottish borrowing than for the UK, at least initially, and there would also be costs for mortgage companies in meeting a separate set of regulations. This has led the Council of Mortgage Lenders and others to say that mortgages are likely to be more expensive in an independent Scotland. If Scotland introduced its own currency, even if that were pegged to sterling, exchange risk would also be involved, since mortgages would still be denominated in sterling, if they were with UK mortgage companies, but the assets (houses and flats) on which the mortgages were based would be denominated in pounds

Scots. This could make the mortgage companies want to reduce their exposure. It would, therefore, be unwise for borrowers to seek funds from companies outside Scotland, unless they had subsidiary offices in Scotland and were prepared to lend in pounds Scots. Those who already had sterling mortgages would need to consider having them redenominated in pounds Scots. Inevitably, this would require major reorganisation in the mortgage market.

Pensions have suffered greatly since 1980 from interference by successive governments of both main UK parties. The Scottish Government have given a commitment that the state pension would continue as at present and that the 'triple lock' would apply throughout the life of the first Parliament after independence. In January 2014, David Cameron gave the same commitment for the next UK Parliament, if he is Prime Minister. This means that the pension would be up-rated each year by the increase in the Retail Price Index for that year, the increase in earnings or 2.5 per cent, whichever is the greatest. In reality, of course, as past history shows, future government interference cannot be ruled out, especially as the state pension is unfunded and pensions take up almost half of the total expenditure on welfare. It will depend on what the priorities of future governments are and what they can afford.

A potentially serious problem could arise with private and company pensions after independence, one which has been highlighted by the Institute of Chartered Accountants for Scotland. The IORP Directive of the EU requires cross-border pensions to be fully funded. Partly as a consequence of government policy, in particular the ending of tax relief by Gordon Brown when Chancellor, but also the movements of the stock market, many pension providers are running with deficits and some companies have got into serious trouble. In time it is expected that these deficits can be eliminated, but that will take some years. If the Directive was strictly applied after independence, there would be a very serious problem and some pension schemes would be forced into insolvency, with considerable loss to pension holders. It would be reasonable to expect that a transition period could be negotiated to allow time for these schemes to become fully funded. It would not seem sensible for this to be a roadblock when the purpose of the Directive was to promote the development of an integrated market in financial services. But, as with other aspects of independence, this would depend on goodwill from other member states.

So there is a lot to think about if Scotland becomes independent – many of the unknowns would depend on the outcome of negotiation. Some of these – the choice of currency, in particular – are of enormous importance. Much could go wrong and it is impossible at this stage to know whether the added flexibility in policy that independence would bring would make Scotland stronger in the long run, or whether people would be worse off. Obviously, it would depend on the wisdom or otherwise of government policies. In the short run, however, substantial cost seems inevitable from breaking the union and introducing new institutions and regulations. This could cause damage to the economy, especially to the financial sector, which would apply even if the Government successfully negotiated monetary union. It would be a bumpy ride at first, and for many people disillusioning, until things got a chance to settle down and those responsible for government learnt what they could and could not do. After Ireland became independent in 1922, it was a long time – at least a generation – before policies were adopted that began to bring the country to the high level of prosperity it was able to achieve and, despite the severe effects of the financial crisis, still has. I would not expect that to happen in Scotland, but it would take some time. There has been a tendency in some quarters to think that North Sea oil revenues will pay for everything. That is clearly not so.

Greater Devolution

At the time of writing, a majority vote for independence in the 2014 referendum looks unlikely, but the polls all show that a large number of voters want to see more powers devolved to the Scottish Parliament. If Scotland is to stay in the UK in the longer term on a basis where the majority of people are content with the constitutional arrangement, something needs to be done to meet these aspirations. The 'Better Together' campaign has been criticised for its inability to say what would be offered in the event of a NO vote in the referendum. All three unionist parties have set up committees to work on proposals, but at the time of writing only Sir Menzies Campbell's Lib Dem committee has produced a report. It is expected that the position will become clearer when the other parties produce their reports, probably in the spring, but whether they will be able to put forward an agreed proposal is probably unlikely. There are, however, possibilities of further devolution both in taxation revenue and in welfare, the main category of expenditure where the Scottish Government's role is limited, as explained in Chapters 2 and 8.

Some of what has been suggested, in Devo-Max, seems to be incompatible with Scotland remaining within the UK. But both the Campbell Committee and the Devo-Plus group argued for entrenching the Scottish Parliament, so that it could not be abolished on a whim of Westminster, thereby making it sovereign in those matters it controls. Moreover, with the Scottish Parliament responsible for so much of the public expenditure in Scotland but up to now without responsibility for tax revenue, other than local authority taxation, there is a clear lack of accountability. The Scotland Act 2012 will improve this, but it would be possible to go further. In Chapter 2, I have suggested devolving three-quarters of Income Tax and assigning the proceeds of VAT, apart from the contribution to the EU. Together with the other smaller taxes in the Scotland Act 2012 and those recommended by Calman but not so far implemented, this would result in over half of the public expenditure of the Scottish Government being funded by taxes paid in Scotland.

I do not favour devolving the whole of Income Tax, as some others have suggested, because it is the main instrument that can be used to affect the distribution of income. It would also be unwise to leave the UK Parliament only with taxes that are regressive if it has to find money for emergency and unforeseen expenditure. Many people regard tax assignment, as I have suggested for VAT, without power to alter rates, as pointless. (EU rules prohibit different rates between parts of one member state.) But it is not pointless to have more of Scottish public expenditure financed by taxes that are paid by the Scottish people. It would mean, if the Scottish Government were able, through its policies, to improve the performance of the economy, it could gain increased revenue. Taxpayers in other parts of the UK might, thereby, be at least a little less concerned than they are at present about the way in which public spending in Scotland is funded, knowing that more than half of the expenditure is paid for by Scottish taxpayers. Such an arrangement would leave Scotland more exposed to fluctuations in revenue, caused by changing economic conditions, and it might be necessary to increase the Scottish Government's power to borrow.

Even with these much greater tax revenues, there would still be a need for a grant to finance the part (nearly a half) of the Scottish Government's expenditure not covered directly by Scottish tax revenue. The Prime Minister has said he has no plans to alter or revise the Barnett formula. I see no alternative to eventually basing this grant on an agreed needs assessment, as no other arrangement is defensible, but the transition to this would need to be planned over a number of years and would be easier when the economy was buoyant than in conditions such as at present.

The Scottish Parliament already has responsibility for the bulk of domestic public expenditure. The one big exception is social security or welfare, where the policy and the bulk of the cost is the responsibility of the UK Department for Work and Pensions (DWP). Several polls have shown that the Scottish people would like to see this responsibility devolved. I do not believe, however, that within a single state it would be acceptable to have different rates of state pension or other benefits that are contributory through national insurance. But Council Tax Benefit is already being devolved and Housing Benefit is another obvious candidate, given the Scottish Government's responsibility for social housing. There are several other benefits – of which the most important in terms of cost is Disability Living Allowance (shortly being replaced by Personal Independence Payments) – that should be considered for devolution and these are listed in Chapter 8. In total these cost £4.5 billion in 2011–12 and comprised almost a third of the DWP expenditure. If responsibility for these benefits were transferred to the Scottish Government, it would give it greater policy flexibility to decide its own priorities. It would also increase its ability to tackle the growth in inequality, which many see as a priority in Scotland. It should be borne in mind, however, that, because of Scotland's demography, the cost of welfare could be a burden that rises more rapidly in Scotland than for the UK as a whole.

A lot can still happen in the months before the referendum. If independence is rejected, however, there is a real danger that politicians at Westminster and officials in Whitehall may think that they can put away the files and not worry about Scotland any more. Proposals for increased devolution might then be shelved. In fact, this is quite a likely outcome and could potentially lead to a feeling of bitterness and disillusion, especially if the 'No' vote had won on a negative campaign that suggested Scotland was too poor or too fearful to embrace independence. It would probably mean that the next time there was a big surge in support for independence in Scotland, maybe in ten or twenty years' time, it would carry the day in a second referendum. That has been the pattern in the past. The 1970s devolution referendum was inconclusive, but 20 years later, after discontent with Scotland's constitutional arrangements had been ignored, there was a clear majority in favour.

I suspect that some at least of the discontent that has led to a desire for independence or more devolution stems from an undefined feeling of injustice as a result of the increasing dominance of London both politically and economically in the United Kingdom. There has been uneasiness that the dominance of the London financial sector has been accompanied by the decline of industries elsewhere, especially manufacturing. This is felt in Scotland despite the fact that the success of the Scottish financial sector is one of the reasons why its economy has performed better than that of other parts of the UK. Many of the industries that once provided the strength of the Scottish economy, however, have disappeared over the last 30 or so years. Even if much of this was inevitable, it was a painful process and has left problems of deprivation in several parts of Scotland. In parts of the north of England and Wales, regions that have done less well economically than Scotland, there has been the same experience.

This points to an urgent need to rebalance the British economy, both geographically and in its structure. The policy of trying to promote growth in the regions outside London, on which much emphasis was laid in the 1960s and 1970s, was greatly weakened in the 1980s, when regional development policy was regarded as no longer in-keeping with the then government's free market philosophy. At the same time, deregulation, including the so-called 'Big Bang', removed most of the previous restrictions on the financial sector. It has contributed much to the economy in both employment and tax revenue but, in 2008, it nearly brought the country to ruin and we are still suffering from the effects. It is time to alter the balance for the sake of all parts of the United Kingdom.

Notes

Chapter 1

1. Scottish Government, *Scotland's Future: Your Guide to an Independent Scotland* (Edinburgh, November 2013).
2. Scottish Executive, *Scottish Abstract of Statistics*, No. 5 (Edinburgh, 1975).
3. The Scottish Office, *Scottish Economic Bulletin* (various years).
4. Scottish Executive, *Scottish Abstract of Statistics*. For estimates of GDP per head in 1960 and throughout the 1950s, see my *Scotland's Economic Progress 1951–1960* (George Allen and Unwin, 1965), pp. 32–6.
5. As reported on 20 March 2013.
6. Scottish Government, *Scotland's Future*, Chapter 3, November 2013.
7. Scottish Government, *Government Expenditure and Revenue Scotland 2011–12* (Edinburgh, March 2013).
8. Alex Kemp, *The Official History of North Sea Oil and Gas* (Routledge, 2012).
9. For Scottish National Accounts Project – see the Scottish Government website.
10. Commission on Devolution in Wales (Silk Commission), *Empowerment and Responsibility: Financial Powers to Strengthen Wales* (Cardiff, November 2012); NI Department of Finance & Personnel, *Northern Ireland Net Fiscal Balance Report, 2009–10 and 2010–11* (Bangor, County Down, November 2012).
11. Scottish Government, *Government Expenditure and Revenue Scotland 2011–12*, p. 45
12. I analysed this subject in detail in 'Scotland's Public Finances from Goschen to Barnett', *Fraser of Allander Institute Quarterly Economic Commentary*, Vol. 24, No. 2 (March 1999).

13. *Central Scotland: A Programme for Development and Growth*, Cmnd 2188 (HMSO, November 1963) and *The North-East: A Programme for Development and Growth*, Cmnd 2206 (HMSO, November 1963).

14. Scottish Government, *Government Expenditure and Revenue Scotland 2011–2012*.

15. Scottish Government, *Government Expenditure and Revenue Scotland 2011–2012*, p. 40.

16. Commission on Scottish Devolution (Calman Commission), *Serving Scotland Better: Scotland and the United Kingdom in the 21st Century* (June 2009); Independent Commission on Funding and Finance for Wales (Holtham Commission), *Fairness and Accountability: A New Funding Settlement for Wales* (Cardiff, 2010).

17. Scottish Government, *Scotland's Future*, p. 69.

18. Oral evidence taken before the committee on 17 April 2012.

19. Scottish Government, *A National Conversation – Your Scotland, Your Voice* (November 2009), p. 38 ff.

20. Jim and Margaret Cuthbert, *Issues Surrounding the Sharing of UK Debt Post Independence*, Jimmy Reid Foundation (January 2014).

21. Michael Amior, Rowena Crawford and Gemma Tetlow, *Fiscal Sustainability of an Independent Scotland*, Institute for Fiscal Studies (November 2013), Chapter 3.

22. Ibid.

Chapter 2

1. HM Government, *Strengthening Scotland's Future*, Cm 7973, TSO (2012).

2. Commission on Scottish Devolution, *Serving Scotland Better: Scotland and the United Kingdom in the 21st Century* (June 2009).

3. HM Government, op. cit., p. 23.

4. HM Government, op. cit., p. 25.

5. HM Government, op. cit., p. 23.

6. HM Government, op. cit., pp. 36–40.

7. Report of a committee under the chairmanship of Sir Menzies Campbell, *Federalism: The Best Future for Scotland* (Scottish Liberal Democrats, 2009).

8. Scottish Government, *A National Conversation – Your Scotland, Your Voice* (November 2009)

9. Available on the website of the David Hume Institute.

10. *Ibid.*

11. Andrew Hughes Hallett and Drew Scott, *Scotland: A New Fiscal Settlement*, GMU School of Public Policy Research Paper (3 June 2010).

12. Reform Scotland, *A New Union* (Edinburgh, Third Report of the Devo-Plus Group, 2012).

13. Report of a committee under the chairmanship of Sir Menzies Campbell, op. cit.

14. Alan Trench, *Devo-More: Fiscal Options for Strengthening the Union* (IPPR, January 2013).

15. EU Energy Products Directive (EPD), Council Directive 2003/96/EC (October 2003).

16. Scottish Government, *Fiscal Autonomy in Scotland* (Edinburgh, 2009).

17. Independent Commission on Funding and Finance for Wales, *Fairness and Accountability: A New Funding Settlement for Wales* (July 2010).

18. Ray Perman, *Hubris: How HBOS Wrecked the Best Bank in Britain* (Birlinn Ltd, 2012).

Chapter 3

1. Scottish Government, *Corporation Tax: Discussion Paper – Options for Reform* (August 2011).

2. Scottish Government, *Scotland's Future: Your Guide to an Independent Scotland* (Edinburgh, November 2013), Chapter 3, p. 120.

3. Scottish Government, *Government Expenditure and Revenue Scotland 2011–2012* (Edinburgh, March 2013).

4. Scottish Government, Fiscal Commission Working Group, *First Report – Macroeconomic Framework* (Edinburgh, 2013).

5. Brian Quinn, *Regulation, Supervision, Lender of Last Resort and Crisis Management* within 'Scottish Independence: Issues and Questions', Hume Occasional Paper No. 99, August 2013.

6. *Irish Times* (9 August 1938).

7. Conor McCabe, *Sins of the Father: Tracing the Decisions that Shaped the Irish Economy* (The History Press, 2011).

8. Scottish Government, Fiscal Commission Working Group, op. cit.
9. Reported in *The Scotsman* (21 February 2013).
10. IMF, *World Economic Outlook* (October 2010).
11. IMF, *Fiscal Monitor Update* (July 2012).
12. Dawn Holland and Jonathan Portes, *Self-defeating Austerity*, National Institute Economic Review, No. 222 (October 2012).

Chapter 4

1. HM Government, *Scotland Analysis: Devolution and the Implications of Scottish Independence*, Cm 8554, (February 2013).
2. John Kerr (Lord Kerr of Kinlochard), 'Don't count on it: Scotland, if independent, could not assume that rejoining the EU would be easy – or cheap', *Prospect Magazine* (23 January 2013). For a fuller version, see the Scottish Constitutional Forum Blog, 30 January 2013.
3. European Commission, *EU Budget 2011: Financial Report* (Brussels, 2012).
4. HM Treasury, *European Union Finances 2012*, Cm 8405 (July 2012).
5. European Commission, op. cit.
6. Committee of Inquiry, *The Future of Scotland's Hills and Islands* (Royal Society of Edinburgh, September 2008).
7. Ibid.
8. The problems of fisheries policy were thoroughly analysed in the report of the Royal Society of Edinburgh, *Inquiry into the Future of the Scottish Fishing Industry* (March 2004), of which I was vice-chairman.
9. Many of these issues were discussed in the Royal Society of Edinburgh, *Inquiry into the Future of the Scottish Fishing Industry* (March 2004).
10. See, for instance, Jean-Claude Piris's excellent book *The Future of Europe* (Cambridge University Press, 2012).

Chapter 5

1. Ray Perman, *Hubris: How HBOS Wrecked the Best Bank in Britain* (Birlinn Ltd, 2012).
2. Robert Peston and Laurence Knight, *How Do We Fix This Mess?* (Hodder & Stoughton, 2012).

3. His readiness to lend is well set out in Robert Peston's *Who Runs Britain?* (Hodder & Stoughton, 2008).
4. Scottish Government, *Scotland's Future: Your Guide to an Independent Scotland* (Edinburgh, November 2013), pp. 112–13.
5. Roger Boyes, *Meltdown Iceland* (Bloomsbury, 2009).
6. David J. Lynch, *When the Luck of the Irish Ran Out* (Palgrave Macmillan, 2010); Conor McCabe, *Sins of the Father* (The History Press, 2011), especially Chapter 5.
7. Final Report of the Independent Commission on Banking, Chairman Sir John Vickers, 12 September 2011.
8. Robert Peston and Laurence Knight, *How Do We Fix This Mess?*, op. cit.
9. The details and comparisons are fully set out in my book with Mark Stephens, *Housing Policy in Britain and Europe* (UCL Press, 1995).

Chapter 6

1. Scottish Environmental Protection Agency, *State of Scotland's Environment 2006* (Stirling, October 2006).
2. Scottish Environmental Protection Agency website, www.sepa.org.uk, *A Climate Change Plan*.
3. Lord Nicholas Stern, *The Economics of Climate Change: The Stern Review* (Cambridge University Press, 2007).
4. Scottish Government, *Energy in Scotland: A Compendium of Energy Statistics* (May 2012).
5. Royal Society of Edinburgh, *Inquiry into Energy Issues for Scotland* (June 2006).
6. Department of Energy and Climate Change, *Energy Trends* (December 2012).
7. Scottish Hydropower Resource Study (2008).
8. Reported in *The Scotsman* (10 January 2013).
9. House of Commons Select Committee on Energy and Climate Change, oral evidence from Dr David Kennedy (19 November 2012).
10. International Energy Agency, *World Energy Outlook 2012*.
11. KPMG International, *Comparison of Shale Gas in the US and CEE* (2012).
12. Royal Society and Royal Academy of Engineering, *Shale Gas Extraction in the UK: A Review of Hydraulic Fracturing* (June 2012).

13. House of Commons Select Committee on Energy and Climate Change, oral evidence from Mr Francis Egan of Cuadrilla Resources (11 December 2012).
14. Royal Society and Royal Academy of Engineering, *Shale Gas Extraction in the UK: A Review of Hydraulic Fracturing* (London, June 2012).

Chapter 7

1. Scottish Government, *Government Expenditure and Revenue Scotland 2011–2012* (Edinburgh, March 2013).
2. This is based on the median line in the North Sea between England and Scotland used in estimates made by Alex Kemp and Linda Stephen of Aberdeen University. Scotland's share depends not only on how the line is drawn but also on the price of oil and the output of particular fields in any one year. See Alex Kemp's memorandum submitted to the House of Commons Select Committee on Energy and Climate Change, Session 2011–2013.
3. For example, *The Observer* on two successive Sundays in February 1974 in the run-up to the election.
4. Alex Kemp, *The Official History of North Sea Oil and Gas,* 2 vols (Routledge, 2011).
5. Ibid.; House of Commons Select Committee on Energy and Climate Change, oral evidence taken on 17 April 2012.
6. HM Revenue & Customs, *Statistics of Government Revenues from UK Oil and Gas Production* (August 2013).
7. Based on OECD figures for GDP (see Chapter 1).
8. Unlike my earlier 1974 paper, this one has not been made public.
9. Scottish Government, Fiscal Commission Working Group, *First Report – Macroeconomic Framework* (2013).
10. Alex Kemp, op.cit, Vol. 1 pp. 584–95
11. As reported in *The Scotsman* (28 February 2013).
12. *The Scotsman* (16 January 2013).

Chapter 8

1. John Curtice and Rachel Ormiston, *Attitudes Towards Scotland's Constitutional Future*, Scottish Social Attitudes Survey (ScotCen, January 2013).

2. David Bell, *Social Protection in Scotland*, a paper for the ESRC, available from the David Hume Institute website.
3. Department for Work and Pensions, *Universal Credit: Impact Assessment (1A)* (December 2012).
4. Jim McCormick's report, *Welfare 'Reform' and Mitigation in Scotland* for the Scottish Council of Voluntary Organisations (January 2013).
5. David Bell, op. cit.
6. Hannah Aldridge, Peter Kenway and Tom MacInnes, *Monitoring Poverty and Social Exclusion, Scotland, 2013* (Joseph Rowntree Foundation, 2013).
7. Jonathan Cribb, Robert Joyce and David Phillips, *Living Standards, Poverty and Inequality in the UK* (Joseph Rowntree Foundation for the Institute for Fiscal Studies, 2012).
8. Ibid.
9. Professor David Bell and David Eiser, *Inequality in Scotland: Trends, Drivers and Implications for the Independence Debate* (University of Stirling Management School, 2013).
10. Ibid.
11. Lesley Riddoch writing in *The Scotsman* has argued for the Scandinavian model and Joyce McMillan for a more equal society.
12. Scottish Government, *Scotland's Future: Your Guide to an Independent Scotland* (Edinburgh, November 2013), Chapter 4, pp. 150–66.
13. The Mirrlees Review, *Tax by Design*, for the Institute for Fiscal Studies (Oxford University Press, 2011).
14. See, for example, Alan Trench, *Funding Devo-More: Fiscal Options for Strengthening the Union* (IPPR, January 2013).

Chapter 9

1. The Council for Mortgage Lenders, http://better.tg/19FYB73.
2. Reported in the *Daily Telegraph* (21 May 2013).
3. HM Government, *Scotland Analysis: Financial Services and Banking*, Cm 863 (May 2013).
4. See Professor Goodhart's chapter in Andrew Goudie (ed.), *Scotland's Future: The Economics of Constitutional Change* (Dundee University Press, 2013), p. 150.
5. ICAS, *Scotland's Pensions Future: What Pensions Arrangements Would Scotland Need?* (April 2013).

6. Scottish Government, *Pensions in an Independent Scotland* (September 2013).

7. NAPF, *Scottish Independence: The Implications for Pensions* (November 2013).

8. HM Treasury, 2010 Budget.

9. Pensions Commission, *A New Settlement for the Twenty-First Century*, Second Report of the Commission (2005), p. 119.

10. Scottish Government, *Scotland's Future: Your Guide to an Independent Scotland* (Edinburgh, November 2013), p. 146.

11. For example, Guaranteed Retirement Benefit, abolished in 1975, still pays out a small amount, and the State Earnings-Related Pension Scheme (SERPS), which was replaced by the State Second Pension in 2002.

12. Scottish Government, *Pensions in an Independent Scotland* (September 2013); also, Scottish Government, *Scotland's Future* (November 2013).

13. HM Treasury, *Independent Public Service Pensions Commission: Final Report by Lord Hutton* (March 2011).

14. Ibid., p. 55.

15. Alex Brummer, *The Great Pensions Robbery: How New Labour Betrayed Retirement* (Random House Business Books, 2011), p. 5.

16. Scottish Government, *Pensions in an Independent Scotland* (September 2013), p. 78.

17. NAPF, op.cit., p. 11.

Index